40 Tools for Cross-Functional Teams

40 Tools for Cross-Functional Teams

Building Synergy for Breakthrough Creativity

Walter J. Michalski, Ed.D.

edited by
Dana G. King, M.A.

Productivity Press • Portland, Oregon

Additional copies of this book are available from the publisher. Discounts are available for multiple copies through the Sales Department (800-394-6868). Address all other inquiries to:

Productivity Press
P.O. Box 13390
Portland OR 97213-0390
United States of America
Telephone: 503-235-0600
Telefax: 503-235-0909
E-mail: service@ppress.com

Cover design by Carla Refojo
Cover illustration by Ana Capitaine
Text design by Janet Brandt and Jonathan Wills
Design additions for this edition by Susan Swanson
Page composition by William H. Brunson, Typography Services
Art creation by Smith & Fredrick Graphics and Jonathan Wills
Printed by BookCrafters in the United States of America
Six Sigma is a federally registered trademark of Motorola.

Library of Congress Cataloging-in-Publication Data

Michalski, Walter J.
    40 tools for cross-functional teams : building synergy for
breakthrough creativity / Walter J. Michalski ; edited by Dana G. King.
        p.   cm.
    "This book contains . . . 40 of the 222 tools that are in the Tool
navigator"—Introd.
    Includes bibliographical references and index.
    ISBN 1-56327-198-2 (pbk.)
    1. Total quality management.   2. Teams in the workplace.
3. Creative ability.   I. King, Dana G.   II. Michalski, Walter J.
Tool navigator.   III. Title.
HD62.15.M527   1998
658.4′02—dc21   98-34170
                                                                           CIP

03 02 01 00 99 98   10 9 8 7 6 5 4 3 2 1

Contents

Contents

Stage Seven: Navigator Tools to Assess Team Creativity

Stage Eight: Navigator Tools for Team Recognition and Reward

Publisher's Message

When discussing what it takes to build effective teams it is apropos to include some analysis as to "why teams fail." We include such a section in this guide because, unfortunately, there are many more team failures than successes. This may be why every few years the issue of building effective teams becomes a hot topic—especially since teams are an *essential* element in developing a world class manufacturing environment. Concepts like TQM, work cells, learning organizations, and using total employee involvement to create effective teams end up in books and seminars about organizational change, lean thinking, and quick response manufacturing, etc. Still, no matter how many excellent seminars, consultants, or books we use in our effort to implement a team environment, we are pursued by that ugly phrase—"why teams fail." Walter Michalski says, "It may be the lack of commitment and resources from the top, or turf and power struggles, or ineffective communications, but the bottom line is that when it comes to creating a successful team environment, the organization is just getting in the way of itself."

In *40 Tools for Cross-Functional Teams—Building Synergy for Breakthrough Creativity*, Walter Michalski cuts through the thicket of team literature and succinctly gleans the do's and don'ts to give us lessons for building and sustaining cross-functional teams. He then gives us 40 carefully-selected tools in the same easy-to-read format found in the *Tool Navigator™—The Master Guide for Teams*. He arranges these tools in eight process stages, from getting teams up and running, through building consensus and synergy, to using idea generating tools to creatively solve problems. This book will assist *any* team configuration in every phase of their evolution. Walter says this book "will provide team members with many solutions to their problem-solving and creative work, and will also enable them to learn about behaviors that will unify and sustain the team, making it an effective and creative force within the organization." It will also help the organization get out of the way so its teams can thrive.

40 Tools for Cross-Functional Teams is the second book in a series of problem-solving and quality/process improvement tool books that Productivity Press is developing based on the *Tool Navigator™*. The first book was *40 Top Tools for Manufacturers—A Guide for Implementing Powerful Improvement Activities*. We are tailoring each of these streamlined tool books to meet the specific needs and areas of interest of problem-solving teams. Future books may focus on customer/quality metrics or change management. Or we may present one or more of the six problem-solving phases; for example, selecting and defining a problem or opportunity, or developing and planning possible solutions or changes. We may even organize a tool book around one of the eight tool classifications such as analyzing/trending or changing/implementing.

In our continuous effort to satisfy our customers we would appreciate any comments you have on *40 Tools for Cross-Functional Teams* so we can provide you with the navigator tools you need, packaged in the way you need them. We are excited about this valuable book. It fills an important need for our customers, which is to enhance the potential of everyone in the organization. We hope to be hearing your stories about "why your team is succeeding." You can contact customer service at 1-800-394-6868, or email us at service@ppress.

Our thanks go to the team that helped develop this latest tool companion; Walter Michalski for his advice in choosing and arranging the tools as they appear in this book; Gary Peurasaari, developmental editor; Mary Junewick, copyeditor, proofreader, and production editor; Janet Brandt and Jonathan Wills, text designers; design additions for this edition, Susan Swanson; Lee Smith of Smith & Fredrick Graphics, art creator; William Brunson of Typography Services, text compositor; Carla Refojo, cover designer; and Ana Capitaine, cover illustrator.

Steven Ott
President and Publisher

Acknowledgments

This book has been "written" by a great number of people who have taught me the various tools and how to use them for cross-functional synergy in a team environment. It has been invaluable to know which problem-solving and creativity tools to apply when faced with specific team problems. I would like to thank the numerous team facilitators, consultants, managers, and trainers for their expert input and recommendations. I wish I could remember all the names of people who so freely gave to me this much appreciated knowledge of team building and tools usage over the last 30 years.

My wife, Giovanna, deserves special thanks for her ongoing support and for taking on an extra share of work since I, again, locked myself in my study for many weeks to write this book. My sincere thanks to my daughter and expert editor, Dana Giovanna King, for her continuous assistance in editing and revising the drafts. My son, Anthony Peter, often helped me with the computer work and gave timely hands-on instructions. Many thanks to him for keeping me online and "teaching an old dog new tricks."

I would like to also thank the originators of many of the tools presented in this book. I have made every effort to identify and credit them and offer my sincere apology if I have overlooked anyone.

Finally, I am indebted to my "team" at Productivity Press. I especially want to thank Gary Peurasaari, development editor, for his help in shaping this manuscript. Also Mary Junewick, who copyedited and managed the production process. They shared their ideas, provided timely technical support, and, therefore, contributed greatly to the completion of this book.

Walter J. Michalski, Ed.D.

Introduction

Coming together is a beginning;
keeping together is progress;
working together is success.
—Henry Ford

As team facilitators, we know it is a lot easier to facilitate experienced and successful teams rather than teams that are floundering because of a lack of direction, confidence, or the right tools. And we also know that if success means significant results, new breakthroughs, or a directly measurable positive effect on the quality or the process the team is trying to improve, then more teams fail than succeed. My experience with the early quality circles to the cross-functional, multidisciplinary teams of today, such as integrated product development (IPD) or *six sigma* teams (see Appendix A for a description of six sigma), is that quite often, in the beginning, teams are highly motivated to improve the whole organization only to come to a screeching halt from lack of support, or resources, or much needed tools. Other teams proudly display flip charts filled with brainstorming ideas only to see them collect dust in some manager's office due to a lack of interest, or assignment to low-level priority. The expected encouragement is simply not forthcoming for the team to follow-up on its ideas and recommendations. Other teams, after some initial successes with quality or process improvement issues, fade away because they lack the important tools training that would enable them to tackle more challenging tasks.

However, you can learn some valuable lessons even when teams do not meet goals. For example, when trying to walk, an infant learns to problem solve when it falls. A team is no different. It also needs to learn how to walk. But too many obstacles and set-backs can destroy its initiative.

The unfortunate situation is that even when organizations are willing to use teams, these teams are often unable to establish the right environment or change the organizational culture to ensure successful cross-functional "teaming." It may be the lack of commitment and resources from the top, or turf and power struggles, or ineffective communications, but the bottom line is that when it comes to creating a successful team environment, the organization is just getting in the way of itself. Eileen Sharpiro (1992) captured it well when she quoted the American philosopher Pogo, who said, "We have met the enemy and he is us." She wisely pointed out that "when the enemy is us, then the solution is also us."

What This Book Does

40 Tools for Cross-Functional Teams—Building Synergy for Breakthrough Creativity provides cross-functional or multidisciplinary teams the tools necessary to do things *right*—from the start. It will provide team members with many solutions to their problem-solving and creative work, and will also enable them to learn about behaviors that will unify and sustain the team, making it an effective and creative force within the organization.

The 40 tools I have selected for this book are from the *Tool Navigator™—The Master Guide for Teams* handbook, also published by Productivity Press (1997), which contains 222 tools. The *Tool Navigator™* provides an easy-to-read format of powerful tools for problem-solving and quality/process improvement activities. The book was a result of my constant search for additional, special, or more appropriate tools to enhance my team facilitation skills in total quality management (TQM) principles, and in continuous process improvement methods for the service and manufacturing environment. In writing *40 Tools for Cross-Functional Teams*, I placed the emphasis on tools for team building, team decision making, and team creativity and innovation. These are the tools that promote and activate the cross-functional synergy in teams.

It will be easier for you to effectively use these 40 tools if you will take time to review the standard format/layout employed in this guide. The following 10 components of each tool are shown in Figure I-1 on pages 4–5.

1. Tool number and name (and acronym, if applicable)
2. Tool *also-known-as* (aka)
3. Tool process classification
4. Tool description
5. Typical application. The classification of the tool suggests the tool's particular process application.
6. Problem-solving phase. Each tool is marked as applicable in one or more of six suggested problem-solving phases.
7. Probable links to other tools in the *Tool Navigator™* (*before* and *after*). Though most of these tools do not appear in this guide, the link box still provides the reader with a list of additional tools available to them. (For a complete description of the tools, refer to *Tool Navigator™.*)
8. Notes and key points.
9. Step-by-step procedure that explains how the team is to use each tool.
10. Example of tool application (the output or result). Realistic source data or a problem/opportunity has been used to produce an expected output in the form of a matrix, sketch, flowchart, diagram, graph, table, map, list, or whatever a particular tool produces.

Note: The *Tool Navigator*™ master guide contains an additional component, "Typically used by." This component gives the most important work disciplines in which the 222 tools are most actively used or applied. These disciplines are research/statistics, creativity/ innovation, engineering, project management, manufacturing, marketing/sales, adminis- tration/documentation, servicing/support, customer/quality metrics, and change man- agement. Since this book contains just 40 of the 222 tools that are in the *Tool Navigator*™ and they are to be used by teams in all disciplines, the "Typically used by" component is not necessary.

Table I-1 (pages 6–7) will help the reader identify, select, and use these 40 tools by clas- sification; for example, TB for team building, IG for idea generating, etc.; and determine in which logical problem-solving phase they are typically used. The tools are arranged alpha- betically and the table matches each tool number in this book (1–40) with the respective tool number in the *Tool Navigator*™ (1–222, shown in parenthesis in the second column). Notice that the 40 tools in this book cover the six problem-solving phases, from selecting and defin- ing a problem or opportunity, to recognizing and rewarding team efforts.

Even though this book has the before and after link box (component 7 of Figure I-1) many of the tools mentioned in it are not included this guide. To find these particular tools see Appendix B: Cross-Reference Index, which alphabetically lists the 222 tools (as well as their *aka's*) as they appear in the *Tool Navigator*™. I have also highlighted other tools in Appendix B to help you link to other supporting tools for team building, decision making, idea gener- ating, and cross-functional synergy. For example, you typically use decision making (DM) tools to reach a team decision or consensus on some issue or proposal. On the other hand, change/implementing (CI) tools can be performed as the team's first activities after they have completed Problem Specification (tool 12). These links to other tools can also give you ideas for creating your own steps to improving your process and teams.

Figure I-2 on page 8 shows the logical groupings of tools in the order that the team may use them. These represent the eight stages in the book and display a natural progression begin- ning with assessing whether the organization is ready to establish teams, through various team activities, through assessing creative output, to rewarding teams. The first four stages illustrate the need for teams to spend time to correctly form and build themselves—*before* get- ting the most out of stage five, consensus/synergy. In stage five teams will further unify them- selves by choosing appropriate change/implementing tools and learning how to work together, as well as with other teams. The flowchart in stage five of Figure I-2 illustrates the concept of consensus (all arrows point in the same direction) and shows that team cohesiveness and

Figure I-1. Sample Two-Page Spread Detailing the Components of Each Tool and Their Intended Use.

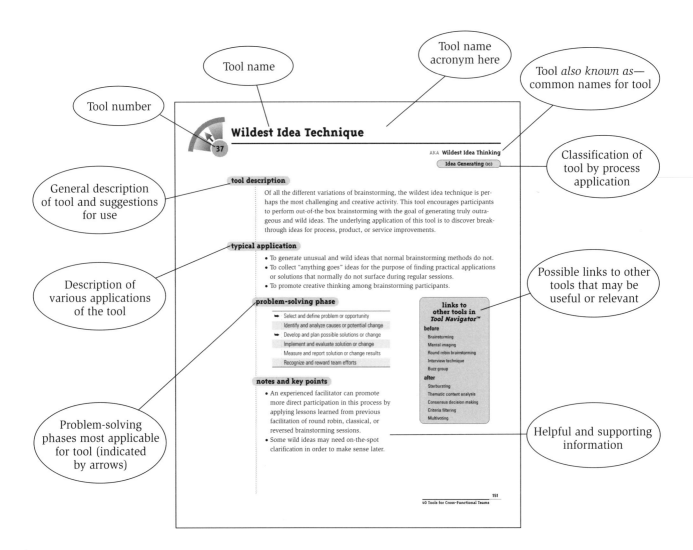

Step-by-step procedure explaining how to use tool

Example of the display, output, or result of the tool's use

TOOL 37   Wildest Idea Technique

step-by-step procedure

STEP 1   The facilitator introduces this brainstorming variation and provides a rationale for using it.

STEP 2   Brainstorming is started by the facilitator's displaying of several outrageous or impossible ideas to a stated topic, issue, or problem. See example *Employee/Team Recognition and Reward*.

STEP 3   Participants generate other wild, crazy ideas or hitchhike on others already mentioned.

STEP 4   The facilitator records ideas on the flip chart and monitors the process closely to ensure that participants do not revert back to generating more conventional ideas.

STEP 5   The process is continued until all participants run out of wild ideas. The final list of ideas is dated and saved for next steps.

example of tool application

Employee/Team Recognition and Reward	Date xx/xx/xx
– Team gets 10% of profits	
– "Honorary Executive" title	
– Team success on E-mail distribution	
– Teams determine recognition/reward	
– Give "markers"	
– Open doors for 2 days	
– Team goes on cruise	
– Job rotation for a week	

– President of the company for a day

Table I-1. Problem-Solving Phases of the Cross-Functional Team Tools (arranged alphabetically)

Classification of Tools

TB	—	Team Building
IG	—	Idea Generating
DC	—	Data Collecting
AT	—	Analyzing/Trending
ES	—	Evaluating/Selecting
DM	—	Decision Making
PP	—	Planning/Presenting
CI	—	Changing/Implementing

Problem-Solving Phases

1. Select and define problem or opportunity
2. Identify and analyze causes or potential change
3. Develop and plan possible solution or change
4. Implement and evaluate solution or change
5. Measure and report solution or change results
6. Recognize and reward team efforts

Tool Number in *40 Tools for Cross-Functional Teams*	Tool Number in *Tool Navigator*™	Class	Tool Name	P-S Phase Number					
				1	2	3	4	5	6
22	(2)	IG	6-3-5 method		•	•	•		
15	(8)	IG	Affinity diagram	•	•	•			
23	(11)	IG	Attribute listing		•	•			
24	(20)	IG	Brainstorming	•	•				
16	(23)	TB	Buzz group	•	•	•			•
25	(27)	IG	Checkerboard method	•	•				
26	(30)	IG	Circle of opportunity		•	•			
2	(32)	TB	Circles of influence		•	•		•	
27	(34)	IG	Circumrelation	•	•				
17	(39)	DM	Consensus decision making	•	•	•			•
38	(48)	ES	Creativity assessment	•	•	•			
18	(50)	IG	Critical dialogue	•	•	•			
39	(67)	PP	Different point of view		•				•
28	(70)	IG	Double reversal	•	•	•			
3	(76)	TB	Fishbowls	•	•	•			
29	(81)	IG	Forced association		•	•			
30	(84)	IG	Fresh eye	•	•	•			
31	(94)	IG	Idea borrowing	•					•
32	(108)	IG	Mental imaging		•	•			
33	(112)	IG	Morphological analysis	•	•	•			
19	(117)	IG	Nominal group technique (NGT)	•	•	•			
4	(125)	TB	Organization mapping	•		•		•	
1	(126)	CI	Organization readiness chart	•	•				
20	(128)	ES	Paired comparison	•		•			
21	(135)	DM	Point scoring evaluation		•	•		•	
40	(139)	PP	Presentation					•	•
12	(145)	PP	Problem specification	•	•				
13	(150)	CI	Process mapping	•	•				
14	(151)	CI	Process selection matrix			•	•		
5	(161)	TB	Relationship mapping	•	•	•			

continued

Table I-1. Problem-Solving Phases of the Cross-Functional Team Tools, *continued*

Tool Number in *40 Tools for Cross-Functional Teams*	Tool Number in *Tool Navigator*™	Class	Tool Name	P-S Phase Number					
				1	2	3	4	5	6
10	(166)	CI	Responsibility matrix			•	•		
11	(169)	CI	Rotating roles		•	•			
34	(174)	AT	SCAMPER	•	•	•			
35	(179	IG	Semantic intuition	•	•				
6	(182)	TB	Sociogram		•	•			
36	(188)	IG	Stimulus analysis	•	•	•			
7	(197)	TB	Team meeting evaluation		•			•	•
8	(198)	TB	Team mirror			•			•
9	(199)	TB	Team process assessment	•	•	•			•
37	(217)	IG	Wildest idea technique	•		•			

synergy must rest on sound decision making by the team. I have carefully selected tools to assist in this process. What comes to my mind is John Parker Stewart's observation (1994) that the word **team** stands for **t**ogether **e**veryone **a**chieves **m**ore.

Once these teams attain cross-functional synergy they are ready to move to stage six and creatively solve problems. Much has been written about the importance of team creativity and innovation. One important piece of advice that keeps coming up is for teams to "step-out-of-the-box" to surface breakthrough process solutions, products, and services. J. Daniel Couger (1995) proposes that creativity programs are the most cost-effective of all programs, even more so than quality improvement programs. He illustrates with a graph that shows the return on investment for creativity to be 300 percent as compared to other investments. This is why I have provided many idea-generating tools for this guide. Some of these such as Checkerboard Method (tool 25), Circumrelation (tool 27), and Semantic Intuition (tool 35) are exceptionally powerful. In stage seven you will apply Creativity Assessment (tool 38) that will assess your teams' progress. But this is not the completion of your team journey. In stage eight you will apply tools that will recognize and reward your teams.

Lessons for Making Cross-Functional Teams Work

All of the tools from stages one through eight, when learned and appropriately used, will make a significant improvement in your team's productivity. But to become truly successful at solving problems, teams must learn how to go from their first baby steps (understanding team concepts) to marathon sprints (applying "teaming" techniques to solve problems). In the remainder of the introduction I will share some important lessons from

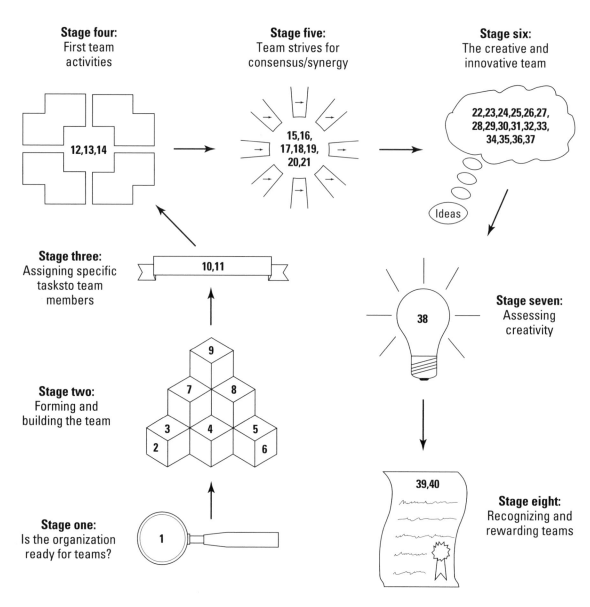

Stage four:
First team
activities

Stage five:
Team strives for
consensus/synergy

Stage six:
The creative and
innovative team

12,13,14

15,16,
17,18,19,
20,21

22,23,24,25,26,27,
28,29,30,31,32,33,
34,35,36,37

Ideas

Stage three:
Assigning specific
tasksto team
members

10,11

Stage two:
Forming and
building the team

9

7 8

3 4 5

2 6

38

Stage seven:
Assessing
creativity

Stage one:
Is the organization
ready for teams?

1

39,40

Stage eight:
Recognizing and
rewarding teams

Note: Tools are sorted and sequenced for a recommended process of application.
Refer to Table I-1 for tool titles and other descriptive information.

Figure I-2. Tools for the Eight Stages of Team Development

people who have been identifying the essential components of successful teams and/or who have made some wise observations about human behavior. I have also included some lessons from a very unlikely source. But first let's take a look at some of the "conventional" wisdom that can help you apply the tools in this book.

A Few Personal Lessons

As an organizational change agent, I have assisted in the establishment and maintenance of teams at different levels in the organization. As a trainer I have trained teams. I have also been asked to help teams that were in trouble. My passion has always been to work with teams—as a contributing team member, a neutral team facilitator, or as a coach and team leader. There are a few simple but powerful lessons that I have learned over time:

- Change is a constant. Constant change makes progress possible.
- The needs of the team are the needs of the organization.
- Researching first prevents redoing later.
- You need to be "alive" for lifelong learning.
- Hear it, learn it, do it.
- Improvement tools help every kind of team.
- Creativity means moving out of the box.
- Committee assessments kill innovative ideas.
- Team recognition and rewards is part of the process.

As I probed the many words of wisdom about teams these same themes seemed to reappear. I have selected the appropriate tools and lessons that will show you the kind of commitment required to build effective teams, teams that are allowed the freedom to apply their creativity to solving problems.

A General Definition of Cross-Functional Teams

Facts often kill a good argument.
—Brian L. Joiner

There are many types of teams. They may function at the problem-solving level on the factory floor or they may consist of several top executives teaming up for the purpose of formulating a vision or strategic goals for the organization. Figure I-3 positions a number of teams, assembled for various purposes, at different levels of an organization. What is a team? Newman and Ketchum, Jr. (1994, p. 75) believe that "whenever a group of people

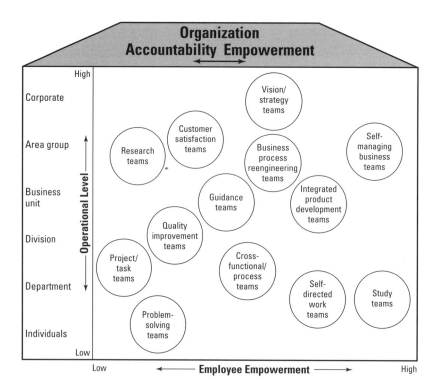

Figure I-3. Purposes and Levels of Teams in the Organization

share responsibility for the decisions that affect all of them, they are a team. Teamwork means contribution and collaboration—it requires both freedom and the ability to participate freely."

We can further identify two basic types of teams: functional and cross-functional. This overview will discuss the establishment and maintenance of cross-functional teams. A cross-functional team, multidisciplinary team, or a self-directed work team whose members consist of employees from various functional departments, are groups of individuals who meet regularly to resolve mutual problems. A definition by Wellins, et al. (1991, p. 3) states that a team is an "intact group of employees who are responsible for a 'whole' work process or segment that delivers a product or service to an internal or external customer."

For example, a cross-functional *six sigma* team would have representatives from marketing, engineering, manufacturing, quality assurance, and other departments, and would have the goal of drastically reducing errors and defects across the organization (see Appendix A for a further discussion of six sigma). This goal naturally requires broad participation and commitment by everyone, including the suppliers! In such a team, all members typically still report to their respective departments, but they also feel tied to the team and share responsibility for team results. Piczak and Hauser (1996, p. 82) say:

> Team members should have a genuine input into substantive decisions that affect their work lives. If employees perceive their participation as being limited to marginal decisions, or worse, that management is simply engaging them in a program of the month, they will regard teams as a naked attempt to get them to work harder. In reality, teams represent a new paradigm of organizational life for both team members and those who interact with them.

Forming a Cross-Functional Six Sigma Team

A problem well stated is a problem half solved.
—Charles F. Katering

Before getting into a discussion of the eight team stages, I want to define what a cross-functional team is in terms of the *six sigma* team. According to McIntosh-Fletcher, "a cross-functional team is comprised of members representing various parts of the formal organization, thus enabling the team to have multiple focuses" (1996, p. 3). This definition pretty much fits a six sigma team, a team consisting of members with diverse expertise called together to change existing processes and methods to achieve six sigma quality.

Briefly stated, to reach a level of six sigma quality, any given process, product, or service should reflect no more than 3.4 defects (or errors) per million opportunities or parts per million. A team with this kind of stretch goal must have representation from planning, marketing, purchasing, design, product engineering, manufacturing, testing, quality assurance, and most important, customers and suppliers. In fact, a team with such a wide overlap slowly changes the organization's culture as they work together to meet this very challenging goal. On the topic of having a culture that support teams, Sherriton and Stern (1997, p. 6) make the following observations:

> The new team culture requires that they contribute, initiate action, ask questions, solve problems, and share responsibility for the success of the team, department, and organization. It requires that they own their behavior and become team players rather than individual experts operating in a vacuum. It means improving their coordination, communications, and decision-making within the context of a department team or multiple

teams. The bottom line is that they must become more accountable for what and how they do things and for sharing responsibility for the culture change . . . the change in culture requires a journey for all organization members.

In addition, "all-way" communication and trust is essential in a six sigma team. Mankin, et al. (1996, p. 248) think that "a lack of trust may be the most daunting boundary of all. It creates inefficiency, blocks commitment, and inhibits change."

Table I-2 displays a generic approach for starting up teams. You can also use this list for a cross-functional six sigma team. A slight modification may be called for in that selected volunteers must have the technical knowledge needed by the team. In addition to the usual just-in-time training, you must provide a six sigma training program to all team members and involve all functional groups to promote effective communications and understanding of the overall process.

The literature further suggests certain guidelines for forming and developing effective teams:

- Teams must have direction and purpose.
- Teams must reflect an egalitarian member status.
- Team members must engage in open communications.
- Team action items must be completed on time.
- Teams must receive training on an as required basis.
- Resources and time must be available to the team.
- Team facilitation and leadership must reflect a participatory management style.
- Team decision making must be via consensus.
- Teamwork and results must be recognized and rewarded.

The above guidelines are certainly true for six sigma teams. Dr. Steven R. Null, Project Manager, Six Sigma, Hughes Electronics, provided me with the following response to questions on team success (1998):

In today's highly competitive business environment, team life spans, business opportunities, and evolving processes are subject to high pressure and rapid changes. Teams can fail for many reasons—perhaps there are as many reasons as there are existing teams. Critical factors like shared purpose, respected and shared leadership, open communications, and a clear definition of tasks are central to successful teams. Any one of these critical factors that is diminished or ceases to function will have a significant impact on team success. Furthermore, for teams to be successful, they must progress toward their goal. This fact is important to both team members and team sponsors.

Table I-2. Steps for Team Start-Up

1. Orientation/awareness training for employees
2. Establishment of a guidance committee
3. Organizational readiness check (by location)
4. Team membership selection from volunteers
5. Team member role assignments
6. Meeting schedule and facility planning
7. Just-in-time training for team, if needed
8. Establishment of team norms
9. Team goals interlock with existing goals
10. Team starts problem solving

Some of the tools in this guide are especially useful to verify that the six sigma team is off to a good start. They will help the team surface the needed adjustments in team behavior, interteam relationships, and team processes. These can be thought of as navigator tools for six sigma:

2	(32)	TB	Circles of Influence
4	(125)	TB	Organization Mapping
5	(161)	TB	Relationship Map
7	(197)	TB	Team Meeting Evaluation
9	(199)	TB	Team Process Assessment

Finally, we need to create measures to check team success. Harrington (1995, pp. 263–264) points out that "no matter the type of team or the problem or issue they are working on, measurement systems must be developed and applied during the start-up of the team. Some simple measurements may be applied to almost any team, regardless of type." Some of his recommended measures are:

• Meeting team milestones
• Proper use of problem-solving tools
• Effective use of time and other resources
• Process cycle-time reductions
• Reject rate reduction, etc.

He goes on to say that "in measuring a team, the important thing is that the team is adding value to the overall organizational improvement effort. The team should be able to prove that they have an important role in improving the performance of the organization, its work environment, product and/or service quality and, very importantly, the people."

After all, it has been said that if you do not measure, you are only *practicing*.

Organizational Readiness

> *Even if you are on the right track,*
> *you get run over if you just sit there.*
> —Will Rogers

Stage One: Navigator Tools to Assess Organizational Readiness contains only one tool, the Organization Readiness Chart. It is the very first tool because it surveys the present organization by asking a number of questions to verify if the organization is ready and capable of implementing a major change effort; namely, the establishment of teams. The completion of the chart will show management the areas they will need to improve to give new teams a chance to succeed.

The establishment of cross-functional teams requires of lot of thought and open communication. The probability of team success depends on the amount of preliminary investigative work performed. I can suggest inverting the pyramid to create a new work ethic of employee empowerment and involvement, or talk of sharing responsibility and risk-taking, as shown in Figure I-4. In reality, however, what manager will, at first glance, openly embrace the role of facilitator, coach, or sponsor—a role that is essential to the support of teams just starting out to change the workplace?

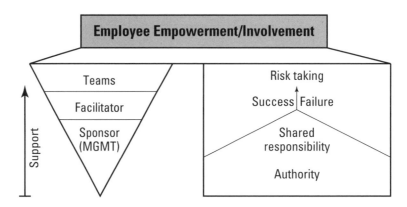

Figure I-4. Instilling a New Work Ethic

In his book review for *Team-Based Organizations*, James H. Shonk (1992) proposes that organizations should consider changing over to teams to give them more of a competitive advantage. He feels (p. 2) that:

Teams require less overhead than traditional organizations and give better service. . . . Teams give an advantage where quality is a major issue, where service is a major issue, and where cost is a major issue—and I don't know any business where those three aren't major issues.

Further, teams offer a way for employees to enrich their work. They no longer have to "park their brains at the door" when arriving at work. These kinds of organizations allow people to make decisions and to function in a way that builds their self-esteem rather than in a way that erodes it.

To help organizations get started, Shonk recommends the following teamwork test (p. 4):

How can you tell if teamwork is right for your organization? Ask these questions:
1. Do employees depend on each other extensively within or across functions or departments?
2. How and where might better coordination (teamwork) enhance your productivity, quality, or customer service?
3. How and where would work teams benefit your organization and employees?
4. How would employees teams fit your firm's long-term goals and strategies?
5. What influence would employee teams have on job satisfaction and employee commitment?
6. How will a team-based organization affect your resources?

I feel that other questions and/or considerations that you need to be aware of are:

- For what purpose will the teams be formed?
- Do the teams' mission and goals support those of the organization?
- What are management's expectations?
- Have team resource and time requirements been placed in the budget?
- How much productive time will be allocated to team schedules?
- Is team membership temporary or permanent?
- What information and training will the team require?
- How will teams report and to whom?
- What level of authority is given to the team?
- Do teams require a guidance team or committee?

The responses to the above questions will provide the information needed to adequately plan and schedule the activities required for team startup. Let us not forget to assign someone to research the do's and don'ts from other organizations' team experiences. Remember, the needs of the team are the needs of the organization!

Team Building for Effectiveness

> *The art of progress is to preserve order amid change*
> *and to preserve change amid order.*
> —Alfred North Whitehead

Team building is the result of a focused change effort that involves an entire section, department, or business unit within the organization. It is management's response to some problem or dissatisfaction. Chances are that the dissatisfaction with the problem must exceed the cost of solving the problem or nothing will be changed. Harrington-Mackin (1994, p. xiv) writes in *The Team Building Tool Kit*:

> Teams have a two-hundred-year history to draw upon for valuable information. Short-lived teams—and yes, there are some—think team building is no more than getting along together. In reality, effective teams build on the vast experiences of others to challenge their members to change their behaviors to accommodate the needs of the team.

Katzenbach (1993a) agrees with this statement. He himself states that "real teams do not have to get along. They have to get things accomplished."

Team building takes time. Fogg (1994, p. 266) acknowledges this by saying:

> It takes at least three years for teams to become effective and for companies to imbed them as way of life for creating change. Organizational buy-in does not happen until teams have proven their effectiveness, team members have been rewarded for their accomplishments, and it is clear even to the skeptics that the company is serious about using teams to drive change.

Dyer (1987, p. 166) is of the same opinion. He feels that one "will not see entrenched behaviors and actions turned around early or easily. . . . One should think of team development as a process that should continue over a period of from one to three years."

The first step in cross-functional or any team building is to perform an organization readiness check (see tool 1 in this guide). The analysis will enable you to resolve organizational problem areas to ensure that your teams have everything they need for a successful start. I feel that no organization will ever be *completely* ready to form teams. Therefore, once you perform the analysis you need to just *do it* (form teams), even if you uncover some weaknesses. Perhaps the newly started team can be assigned to resolve some of these discovered problems as a way of gaining some immediate "teaming" experience. Harrington-Mackin (1994, p. 23) claims she has "seen no significant difference between starting with a strong or weak department, because both will need to learn a very new and different set of skills." Still, it is important to know what your *weak* points are.

There is one other important factor you need to consider in the early phase of team building. This is trust. John Zenger, et al. (1994, p. 37) have this to say on the issue of trust:

> In the team-oriented workplace, by contrast, trust is fundamental. A team won't fulfill its promise unless you can trust the team to follow through on commitments. And you won't fulfill your promise unless the team can trust you to respect them and their ideas.

Right from the team's "forming" stage, change agents, team coordinators, team facilitators, team leaders, and members must review the literature on teams to understand team theory. To complete their research they must discover what works through their own training. And finally, they must start their meetings by practicing what they have learned. Organizational or team learning requires theory, research, and practice on an ongoing basis. Figure I-5 illustrates this concept.

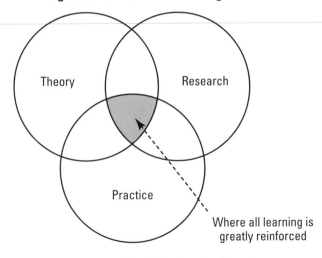

Organizational/Team Learning

Figure I-5. The Synergy of Combining Learning Strategies

Since I mentioned a team "forming" stage, perhaps I should say more about other stages in the team building process. The most familiar "team-maturing" model was proposed by Tuckman (1992) and was developed on the basis of organization studies conducted in 1977. Tuckman believes that teams naturally move through five stages:

1. Forming (team startup)
2. Storming (conflict and competition)
3. Norming (cooperative teamwork)
4. Performing (results and solutions)
5. Adjourning (team goal achievement)

To facilitate the process of moving through these stages, I have selected several team building tools, which include the six sigma tools. Tools 2 through 14 cover stages two, three, and four in this book. These are the tools you will want to use early in the team's problem-solving activities. The full description that introduces each tool will provide the team with enough information to select and appropriately apply the tools.

Stage Two: Navigator Tools for Team Building and Effectiveness

2	(32)	TB	Circles of Influence
3	(76)	TB	Fishbowl
4	(125)	TB	Organization Mapping
5	(161)	TB	Relationship Map
6	(182)	TB	Sociogram
7	(197)	TB	Team Meeting Evaluation
8	(198)	TB	Team Mirror
9	(199)	TB	Team Process Assessment

Stage Three: Navigator Tools for Team Member Assignment

10	(166)	CI	Responsibility Matrix
11	(169)	CI	Rotating Roles

Stage Four: Navigator Tools for First Team Activities

12	(145)	PP	Problem Specification
13	(150)	CI	Process Mapping
14	(151)	CI	Process Selection Matrix

In regard to overall team effectiveness, Scholtes (1988, pp. 6.10–6.22) provides us with a suggested list of ten ingredients for successful teams:

1. Clarity in team goals
2. An improvement plan
3. Clearly defined roles
4. Clear communications
5. Beneficial team behaviors
6. Well-defined decision procedures
7. Balanced participation
8. Established ground rules
9. Awareness of group process
10. Use of the scientific approach

A final word from Evans and Lindsay (1996, p. 453) emphasizes the importance of organizational teamwork: "Employees who participate in team activities . . . were found to feel more empowered, were more satisfied with the rate of improvement in quality in their companies, and were far more likely to have received training on both job-related and problem-solving/team building skills."

Management Support for Team Success

> *There is nothing more difficult to take in hand,*
> *more perilous to conduct, or more uncertain in its success*
> *than to take the lead in the introduction of a new order of things.*
> *Because the innovator has for enemies all those who have*
> *done well under the old conditions, and lukewarm defenders*
> *in those who may do well under the new.*
> —Niccolo Machiavelli

Without ongoing support from top management, teams will fail. According to Robie (1997, pp. 98–101), management must nurture teams through their life cycles, which he defines as conception, birth, adolescence, adulthood, old age, and passing on. In "Is Your Organization Spooked by Ghostly Team Performances?" he provides a well-stated message to management about team support:

> Ensure that your teams have a charter with a clear statement of the opportunity; a methodical process to follow; a measurement system for achievement; resources, constraints, and conditions that will allow for recognition and reward; and a planned disbandment when the team reaches and exceeds its goals.

What do you see when you look at your organization's teams? Are there invisible ghosts rattling chains in the hallways and moaning in the conference rooms, or do you have vibrant teams that are confident in their directions and proud of their achievement paths? Do not let your organization be spooked where it has the ability to be a high performer, and do not allow your team efforts to fade away. Let them flourish and then go out with a fulfilling and rewarding bang. With successful teams, your organization will boost operational performance and improve company culture.

In *Cross-functional Teams*, Glenn Parker (1994) determined the needs of cross-functional teams to be information, resources, and support groups. He further suggests that support should come "in an easy, no-hassle manner and in a professional and timely fashion. On the other hand, if the team has to fight for the support it needs to get the work done quickly, to get it done correctly, then the whole process breaks down" (p. 95). He feels strongly that management should "talk the talk" and "walk the walk."

How important is timely and effective team support? Desler (1997) mentions the results from a 1990 survey completed by DDI, AQP, and *Industry Week* that provide some insight to this question (see Table I-3).

Table I-3. Barriers to Self-Directed Teams

Type of barrier	% of respondents mentioning each
Insufficient training	54
Supervisor resistance	47
Incompatible systems	47
Lack of planning (implementation was too fast)	40
Lack of management support	31
Lack of union support	24

Notes: Respondents could mention more than one category.

Since team support comes mostly from top management, what happens when a team consists of top managers and the information, time, and resources are freely and promptly available? When a team at the top succeeds, Jon Katzenbach (1993b, pp. 230–233) explains it this way:

A discernible pattern emerges with respect to their assignments, approach, and contribution, including:

1. Carving out team assignments that tackle specific issues.
2. Assigning work to subsets of the team.
3. Determining team membership based on skill, not position.
4. Requiring all members to do equivalent amounts of real work.
5. Breaking down the hierarchical pattern of interaction.
6. Setting and following rules of behavior similar to those used by other teams.

The above pattern of success can result only when a team (1) receives an allocation of resources, (2) has access to necessary information, (3) has their predicted team expenses budgeted, and (4) is accorded meeting time to perform effectively within established team goals.

Why So Many Teams Fail

> *The most practical advice for leaders*
> *is not to treat pawns like pawns,*
> *nor princes like princes,*
> *but all persons like persons.*
> —James MacGregor Burns

Recently I asked a friend, Jerold Tucker, assistant vice president, Learning Solutions, GTE, why so many teams fail. It seems that many teams do not succeed or even come close to our expectations, but we do not talk about this since our culture emphasizes and rewards only successful activities. This saddens me when I think of all the powerful lessons we could glean by sharing information about why teams failed. Finding the common patterns and obstacles that lead to team failure would help us avoid repeating the "mistakes" made by others. Here is Tucker's response (1998):

> Generally, teams fail for one simple reason—they do not start as teams. They start as someone's idea to form a team, but they never build the commitment, skills, and consensus that is necessary for teams to win. There is no single purpose for the team, no commitment that they must succeed. Secondly, and equally important, teams fail because whoever forms the teams puts them together to do whatever they are commissioned to do without ever giving them the necessary training and teaming experience they need up front. It would be like

a group of very good athletes being assembled and told their goal is to win a football game. No training, no understanding of why, or what a football game is, and no agreement on what each one will do to contribute to winning the game. If they win, it probably has more to do with individuals and less with the team, and a good deal of luck plays a part in it.

Of course there is not one single cause for why teams fail. You will find many causes if you take the time to analyze beyond the obvious symptoms. Much of your assessment will depend upon how you define team *failure*. My experience shows that close to 50 percent of active teams did not produce or show a significant result after spending considerable time in team meetings, on research and data collection, and on various other problem-solving activities. Robbins and Finley (1995, p. 101) state that "if your team is having difficulties, the odds of leadership being at the root of the difficulties is high." Another interesting comment is given by Harshman and Phillips (1994, p. 156) who point out that "operational barriers arise from pressure to show results, redistribution of power and control, and redistribution of turf and territory."

Managers and team leaders are often uncertain of their role and the proper approach to be taken in managing teams. Albright and Carr (1997, pp. 199-206) in *101 Biggest Mistakes Managers Make* mention, among others, the following mistakes:

- Trying to build a team as a traditional supervisor would do it.
- Not developing commitment to the team's mission.
- Dealing with team members solely as individuals.
- Not developing and living by the team norms.
- Pushing the team to make decisions too quickly.
- Not supporting the team.
- Trying to prevent the team from surfacing and resolving conflict.

Pertinent information comes from a 1995 Hay Group team-based pay survey that included a question of why teams fail. The analysis of the responses with their respective percentages is shown in Table I-4.

Two other frequently mentioned reasons why teams fail are (1) the lack of clearly stated mission, goals, and team objectives; and (2) the absence of a challenging but fair set of measures directly linked to the team's goals or objectives. Figure I-6 reflects a suggested hierarchy of measures for all levels of the organization. Measurement is most effective if the team members are given the autonomy to develop their own measures and arrive at consensus as to how and how often they want to measure their team's performance and progress.

Table I-4. Why Teams Fail

Type of barrier	% of respondents
Goals not clear	35
Changing objectives	35
Inadequate management support	26
Ineffective team leadership	20
Inadequate team member priority	19
No mutual accountability	17

Notes: Respondents could mention more than one category.

As you can see, the review of the literature offers many reasons why teams fail. I have sorted and grouped potential pitfalls and causes into a watch list for team leaders and managers in the organization, and for team training activities (see Figure 1-7). Teams can review this watch list from time to time to see if any of these "team busters" are lurking. Check off the ones that pertain to your team and or company and add up the score.

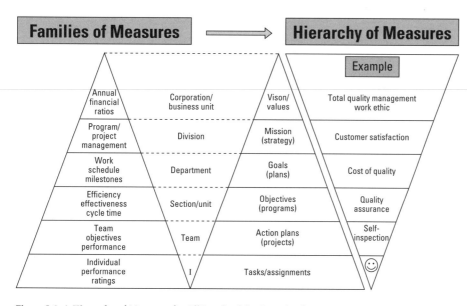

Figure I-6. A Hierarchy of Measures for All Levels of the Organization

---

Walt's Team Buster Watch List

Lack of planning and preparation

☐ Teams are rushed into existence.

☐ No substantial planning takes place before starting or expanding team activities.

☐ There is a rush to accomplish without careful evaluation and planning.

☐ There is little concern for ongoing team development.

☐ Employees do not understand empowerment.

☐ People-building is not emphasized.

☐ Appropriate team training is not provided at all levels.

☐ Teams have insufficient "tools and techniques" skills.

Your score is _____ out of a possible 8 team busters.

Roles and practices

☐ There is excessive control from outside the team.

☐ Existing policies and procedures are barriers for the team.

☐ Members' roles and responsibilities lack proper definitions.

☐ There are unresolved roles.

☐ Decisions are made by authority rule or majority vote.

☐ There are dominating, overbearing team members.

☐ There is an ill-conceived reward system.

Your score is _____ out of a possible 7 team busters.

Vision, goals, and team objectives

☐ There is bleary vision.

☐ Goals or expectations are unrealistic.

☐ Mission, goals, and tasks are unclear and are not shared by all team members.

☐ There are confused goals and cluttered objectives.

☐ There are divergent views, interests, and goals.

☐ Members place priority on individual objectives instead of team objectives.

Your score is _____ out of a possible 6 team busters.

Lack of support

☐ There is no leadership from the top.

☐ Management is not actively and visibly supportive.

Figure 1-7. Assessing Causes of Team Failure

☐ Management does not empower teams to focus on problems and issues.
☐ There is no commitment to the change process.
☐ There is lack of trust.
☐ No substantial effort is made to sell employee involvement.
☐ Insufficient feedback and information are given.
☐ No functioning steering committee oversees the team efforts.
☐ The team lacks timely support or resources.
☐ Team leadership or facilitation is absent.
☐ The team engages in "wanderlust."
☐ There is no team facilitator to serve as a process coach.
☐ Inadequate time is set aside for team activities.

Your score is _____ out of a possible 13 team busters.

Teaming
☐ The team is too large or has high turnover.
☐ There is a lack of risk taking.
☐ The team is not focusing on one problem at a time.
☐ The organization is not open to paradigm shifting.
☐ There is unquestioned acceptance of opinions or alleged facts.
☐ There is inadequate documenting of the progress.
☐ The team lacks an active coordinator.
☐ There are mismatched needs within the team.
☐ There are personality conflicts.
☐ Team members exhibit a lack of concern for one another.
☐ Team members do not attend meetings on a regular basis.
☐ Some team members are feuding.
☐ Team members are not interdependent.
☐ Individual team member orientation is self-serving.
☐ Team members do not complete all steps of a prescribed process.
☐ Team members are considered unproductive.

Your score is _____ out of a possible 16 team busters.

Some of these "infractions" are worse than others, but if you checked 20 or more (40% or over) of the 50 possible team busters you need to begin at stage one in this book.

Team Communications and Cross-Functional Synergy

The most important thing in communication
is to hear what isn't being said.
—Peter Drucker

Organizations of today have accepted the trend toward increased employee involvement and team building. Peter Senge, et al. (1994, p. 354), stated in *The Fifth Discipline Fieldbook:*

> History has brought us to a moment where teams are recognized as a critical component of every enterprise—the predominant unit for decision making and getting things done. Nonetheless, most aspects of existing infrastructure . . . have not yet "captured" the significance of teams. And many people who espouse the importance of teams still believe, when push comes to shove, that the key unit of effectiveness is the individual. This will inevitably change.

Organizations benefit directly from the establishment of cross-functional teams in that these teams address what world class organizations have been doing for some time. World class organizations operate with:

1. *Employee empowerment.* Employees at all levels of the organization are empowered by management and by specifically written organizational practices to participate in the decision-making process related to their position and work. This results in:
   - Increased sense of involvement, belonging, and interdependence.
   - Increased worker motivation level and, therefore, improved morale.
2. *Synergy.* This occurs when team members, working together, produce more than if they were working on their own. It is a smooth interaction among team members and outside persons. All-way communications, trust, mutual support, and team cohesiveness create a "can do" attitude for all. This reflects in:
   - Enhanced team creativity with a greater likelihood that breakthrough concepts will result from team interaction.
   - Increased alignment of efforts among cross-functional teams with less waste in the system.

Another definition of synergy is offered by Ron Willingham, (1997). In *The People Principle* he suggests that "teamwork is essential for getting more done through people. People maximize their potential when they work together in a spirit of unity and harmony toward a common goal or purpose. When they do, a power develops that is greater than the sum of the individual's powers. It is called synergy" (p. 219).

Management can create alignment by influencing team direction, says Kern (1997, p. 111). She suggests that "if teams do not align their efforts and work with the organization's goals and objectives, the organization cannot achieve its required results." Rosabeth Moss Kanter (1989) is also very supportive of this view. In her HBR article "New Managerial Work," she calls for managers to be in the business of "brokering interfaces instead of presiding over employees." I have attempted to create this kind of alignment for cross-functional teams (see Figure I-8). My model includes seven components that must interact to bring about the synergy that a cross-functional team requires to excel. This model discusses team dynamics and team needs and also points out the required communications, interfaces, and support from outside the team.

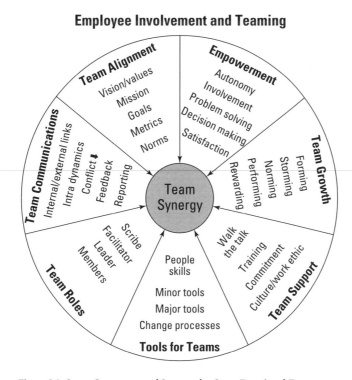

Figure I-8. Seven Components of Synergy for Cross-Functional Teams

Although Felkins, et al. (1993, p. 183) talk about change management, the same considerations and issues apply to achieving cross-functional synergy:

> Effective change management encourages teamwork as a way of linking resources, integrated goals, and involving people in learning together and exchanging competencies. This means developing authentic relationships with trust, openness, mutual respect, and reciprocity. Teamwork not only includes groups inside the formal organizational structure, but also relationships with suppliers, distributors, customers, and community leaders within an expanded and interrelated system.

Cross-functional teams would benefit from having a "boundary manager." According to Kimball Fisher (1993), this manager (1) brings groups together and facilitates a joint problem solving process, (2) is a broker in business training, (3) provides relevant resources or information from external sources, and (4) focuses on customer requirements, vendor issues, quality standards, and interfaces with other teams.

No discussion on team synergy should end without emphasizing the important role that communications play. First, we must have an "atmosphere of honesty and openness," say Willcocks and Morris (1997, p. 18). "The hallmark of an excellent team is its members' ability to say what they think or feel without putting other people down or being put down themselves."

Effective all-way communications is especially needed when many types of teams work at different levels in the organization. I have facilitated numerous types of teams: Type I: Functional Improvement, Type II: Process Redesign, and Type III: Business Rethinking (Mundt, 1994). Unfortunately, I've often encountered the problem of duplication or waste when a higher level team reengineers out the process that was just improved by a lower level team. This happens because of a lack of timely or effective communications.

A desirable aspect of team communications occurs when agreement is reached in the team's decision-making process. Teams often use two ways of making decisions, (1) voting (majority rule) or, (2) consensus. By far, consensus is better for making decisions because all team members have agreed to support an issue or decision. Even if a decision turns out not to have been the best one, dissenting members must refrain from saying that they knew all along it would turn out badly. The team is united on every decision it makes, and the team's synergy is a reflection of how well the decision-making process works. To reach consensus, Rees (1991, p. 152) tells teams to "share ideas, discuss and evaluate, debate, organize and prioritize ideas, and struggle to reach the best conclusion together." Consensus decision making takes considerable time and patience, but a consensus decision is far superior to any other type of decision reached by the team.

There are several tools that help a cross-functional team manage overall team communications, reach team agreement, and make team decisions. For this purpose, I have included the tools in stage five. They contain enough variety for the team to be able to match a specific tool to a particular situation. A brief scanning of the tool descriptions will give you enough information to select the appropriate tool:

Stage Five: Navigator Tools for Team Consensus and Synergy

15	(8)	IG	Affinity Diagram
16	(23)	TB	Buzz Group
17	(39)	DM	Consensus Decision Making
18	(50)	IG	Critical Dialogue
19	(117)	IG	Nominal Group Technique (NGT)
20	(128)	ES	Paired Comparison
21	(135)	DM	Point Scoring Evaluation

Another type of consensus is "group think." Kayser (1994) calls "group think" consensus in excess. This decision-making process may lead to undesirable consequences and, therefore, must be avoided by a cross-functional team. Kayser defines "group think" as a style of deliberation that members use when their desire for concurrence overrides the good sense to evaluate the options available to them. He gives five symptoms of group think (p. 128):

1. The illusion of invulnerability
2. Whitewash of critical thinking
3. Direct pressure
4. Negative stereotypes of the opposition
5. Mind guarding (their mind is made up)

Conflict resolution is also a major component of synergy. Conflict can be healthy if it serves the purpose of airing different opinions on a topic or solution, or if it promotes arguments that will eventually result in team consensus. But other types of conflict may destroy the team's harmony and, therefore must be dealt with. A method of managing team conflict is presented by Harrington-Mackin (1994, p. 64). This method attempts to reduce and stop conflict before it gets out of control:

> Most people have considerable difficulty surfacing and working through problems and conflicts. They "collect stamps"—or little injustices—for long periods of time and use passive-aggressive tactics (procrastination, perfectionism, stubbornness, sniping) to surface

their difficulties. In teams, group conflict cannot be shoved under the rug. Process observers must be empowered by the team to surface conflicts and problems while they are still minor in proportion. A simple wave of the help/hinder list has been known to bring behavior back in line.

As a cross-functional team facilitator, I have used the following principles with great success. Team facilitators, team leaders, and team members should use this practical 8-step win-win strategy to prevent, manage, or resolve team conflict:

1. Ensure that team members understand the conflict issues.
2. Restate the team's common goals and action objectives.
3. Search for other options that the team can agree on.
4. Help the team perform a force field analysis (see tool number 80 in the *Tool Navigator™*). All restraining forces are identified and the team agrees how to deal with them.
5. Develop a list of action items and make assignments to team members.
6. Summarize what needs to be done to eliminate the conflict.
7. Thank the team for their efforts to reach agreement.
8. Consider this conflict resolution a lesson learned to be shared with the team.

Teams Need a Variety of Tools to Perform Well

> *If a hammer is your only tool,*
> *all problems begin to look like nails.*
> —Anonymous

It is time to discuss my favorite topic: tools for teams. It does not make any difference which type of team, for what specific purpose the team has been assembled, or how much experience team members as a collective whole bring to the meeting table; every team will engage in problem solving and will use tools, whether it is to enhance the existing process and quality improvement efforts. or to create new products and services.

Shewhart's cycle of plan-do-check-act (PDCA) is the widely accepted sequence of the continuous improvement process (see Figure I-9). I have added a Venn diagram that displays the overlapping and interacting resource requirements that must be available to ensure organizational success. As a first step, people must have tools to establish and develop teams. Then teams then must have sufficient time to be trained and become active in the various team activities. It all comes down to what I call the three "T's" for problem solving (tools, teams,

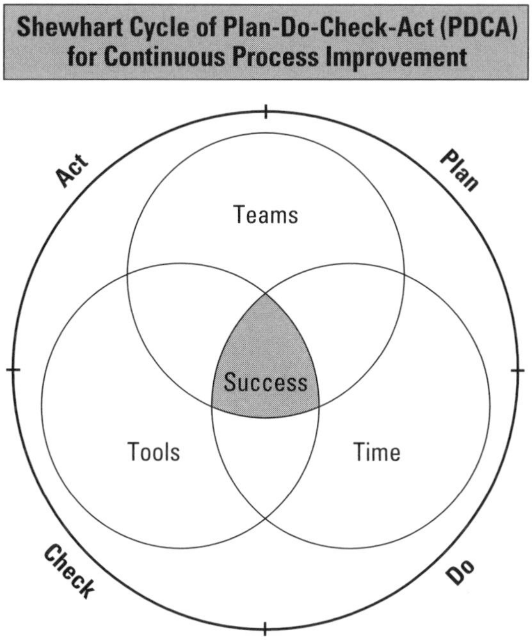

Figure I-9. The Three T's and Continuous Improvement

and time). Of the three components, time may be the most critical, since time waits for no one and once you lose it, you can never recapture it.

Behind every successful cross-functional team is an ongoing training effort. It is absolutely necessary for teams to learn and *practice* the tools in order to have the skills needed to generate ideas and problem-solve, and also to deal with conflict and other team dynamics that involve interpersonal and interfunctional relationships. An exceptionally well-thought-out plan for team training is presented by Aubrey and Felkins (1988, p. 54):

What		*Who*
General orientation		
Introduction	→	All members of the organization
Core training		
Problem solving	→	Leaders
Management presentations	→	Facilitators
		Employee teams

Specialized training

Communication	→	Leaders
Group dynamics	→	Facilitators
Group leadership	→	Facilitators

Advanced training

Special Training	→	Leaders
		Facilitators
		Employee teams

V. Daniel Hunt in *Quality in America* (1992) suggests that awards be given to "excellent teams" as a reward for using "quality first" tools to achieve outstanding results. He includes the use of tools in his three criteria that he feels "makes an excellent team" (p. 230):

1. *Teamwork.* How well does the team work together? Team members on an excellent team (1) understand their purpose as a team, (2) start with a clear problem statement and/or desired output, (3) organize for maximum effectiveness, and (4) use interactive skills well and consistently.
2. *Use of quality tools and processes.* Effective teams (1) use applicable analytical tools, (2) identify several possible alternatives to solving a problem, and (3) evaluate the results of their actions.
3. *Results.* The team project should (1) produce tangible business results, (2) impact the external customer or those who support the external customer, (3) demonstrate an innovative approach, and (4) effectively maximize the cost of quality opportunities.

Any proposed plan for a training program will contain, at its core, many of the tools listed, described, and exemplified in the *Tool Navigator™—A Master Guide for Teams*. I must give one word of advice: to greatly increase the effectiveness of any tools training, it must be presented just-in-time—use the tool only when it is needed. Team members will, without immediate application and practice of the tools, soon forget which tools to use, when to use them (appropriateness and effectiveness), and how to utilize tools in the team setting (skill and efficiency). Helping your team members cross the bridge from theory to practice is the sign of a good training program.

Shewhart Cycle of Plan-Do-Check-Act (PDCA) for Continuous Process Improvement

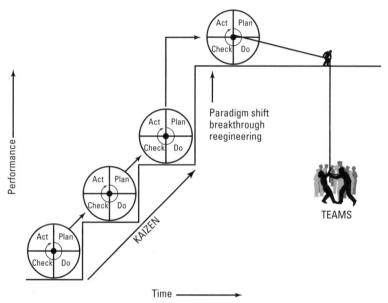

Figure I-10. Improving Operational Results

Enhancing Team Creativity and Innovation

Imagination is more important than knowledge.

—Albert Einstein

For many organizations, the time has come—after years of promoting a work ethic of employee involvement, quality, and process improvement—to raise their expectations that teams be more creative and innovative. The Random House dictionary defines "creative" as: (1) having the power of creating, and (2) resulting from originality of thought or expression. It defines "innovate" as: to introduce something new.

Shewhart's cycle of plan-do-check-act for continuous process improvement (also known as kaizen) has worked well. Today, however, many organizations look for a paradigm shift or a reengineered process that will drastically improve operational results as shown in Figure I-10.

So how can organizations help their teams take one step out of the box and be more creative? Francis and Young (1979, p. 107) claim that:

Creativity does not have to be unplanned and haphazard. Individuals and teams can enhance their creativity by relatively straightforward techniques. We see the creative process as beginning with the identification of a need and the perception of the "missing links." Then a new idea is needed . . . the creative process can be briefly outlined in four steps, as follows: (1) identifying the missing link, (2) generating germs of ideas, (3) developing mature proposals, and (4) testing proposals and absorbing the new idea.

Risk cannot be eliminated from creativity, and the most highly trained and experienced people continue to make errors. Accordingly, hand in hand with creativity must go a mature capacity to make decisions.

In *The Creative Edge*, William Miller (1986, p. 148) gives teams a great recommendation to become more creative: Improve your organization's meetings. He suggests that:

Effective meetings, especially for creative idea generation and problem solving, can be a real pain or pleasure, depending on the skill and sensitivity with which they are conducted. Managing your meetings properly can make a huge difference in the emotional energy you invest in seeing an idea through to completion. Conducting your creative sessions with solid preparation and a variety of idea stimulation techniques can enhance the quality and quantity of alternatives arising from the very different perspectives in your group. It takes practice and diligence, but it's well worth it. Go for it.

To assist team members in their striving for more creativity and innovation, Arieti (1976, pp. 376–377) thinks that a "requirement for the creative person that is even more difficult to accept is gullibility . . . a willingness to explore everything: to be open, innocent and naive before rejecting anything."

A very good friend of mine for many years, Naga Kumar, Ph.D., who is President of Organizational Change Performance, has often talked to me about his 4S model for creativity (1998). Companies can improve the efficiency and effectiveness of their product development processes by using surfacing-selecting-shaping-selling—the 4S model (see Figure I-11).

Surfacing is the process by which employees are motivated and given incentives to increase the generation of ideas for new products. *Selecting* is the process by which management chooses and funds ideas for new products for further development (usually until the prototype is produced and market tested). *Shaping* is the process by which a new product prototype is mass manufactured. *Selling* is the process by which opportunities are created for customers to buy new products and provide feedback on their product use

The 4-S Model

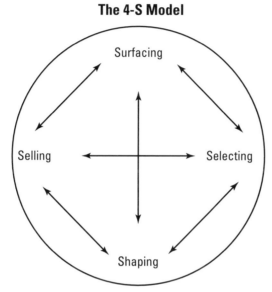

Courtesy of Naga Kumar, Organizational Change Performance

Figure I-11. Improveming Operational Results

experience. The 4S model provides management with a tool to be proactive in helping their organizations place new products in the market and gain first mover advantages.

To help you boost your team creativity, I have carefully selected many idea generating tools for stage six.

Stage Six—Navigator Tools for Team Creativity and Innovation

22	(2)	IG	6-3-5 Method
23	(11)	IG	Attribute Listing
24	(20)	IG	Brainstorming
25	(27)	IG	Checkerboard Method
26	(30)	IG	Circle of Opportunity
27	(34)	IG	Circumrelation
28	(70)	IG	Double Reversal
29	(81)	IG	Forced Association
30	(84)	IG	Fresh Eye
31	(94)	IG	Idea Borrowing

32	(108)	IG	Mental Imaging
33	(112)	IG	Morphological Analysis
34	(174)	AT	SCAMPER
35	(179)	IG	Semantic Intuition
36	(188)	IG	Stimulus Analysis
37	(217)	IG	Wildest Idea Technique

These tools cover both systemic or random association techniques for producing ideas. At first teams may show slow progress with these tools. This is to be expected since some of these tools require concentration, or thinking wildly, or matching and evaluating many different combinations of terms, elements, issues or concepts to produce a breakthrough idea. My advice: Go slowly. Do not take any process shortcuts or you may miss a great idea. Peter Drucker once said, "Every organization needs one core competence: innovation." It is certain that the tools provided in this guide will help cross-functional teams sharpen this competence. Finally, Parker (1994, p. 23) proposes:

Cross-functional teams can be a vehicle for fostering creativity if:
- The culture supports informal problem solving.
- Risk taking is encountered and rewarded.
- Product and service innovations are seen as critical to the organization's future.

Creativity Assessment (tool 38) appears in **Stage Seven: Navigator Tools to Assess Team Creativity**. After your team has brainstormed and come up with creative ways to tackle a problem or process they can assess their effectiveness with this tool.

Recognizing and Rewarding Your Teams

> *There is no limit to what can be accomplished*
> *if it doesn't matter who gets the credit.*
> —Joe Mullins

Much has been written about the basic steps of problem solving. There are models that suggest an approach, or flowcharts that guide teams through the process. Unfortunately, many overlook the important final activity, which is to recognize and reward the team. Table I-5 includes this important step.

I have seen many successful teams receive their just share of bonus money, write-ups, and other formal recognition. But other teams that worked just as hard, used the proper tools,

Table I-5. Problem-Solving Steps with an Essential Last Step

1. Select and define problem or opportunity
2. Identify and analyze causes or potential change
3. Develop and plan possible solutions or change
4. Implement and evaluate solution or change
5. Measure and report solution or change results
6. Recognize and reward team efforts

and performed well, but were able to only validate current processes, products, or services, instead of significantly improving them, did not receive any recognition or reward. How unfair the whole system must have seemed to them! I feel strongly that every team should be rewarded regardless of the final bottom line result. This would certainly maintain a high level of team spirit and motivation throughout the organization. According to Harrington (1995, pp. 470–471):

> Recognition and reward systems must be designed to be compatible with the culture and personality of the organization. It is also important to have teams involved in the design process from the beginning. The key concern is that there must be sufficient reason for the recognition and reward, otherwise the reward system will lose its significance. Recognition and rewards must be part of an overall business plan with budget allocations assigned and honored. There should not be any bureaucratic strings attached; the process must move swiftly through the organization since a recognition and reward loses merit if not given immediately.

On the subject of rewarding cross-functional teams, Parker (1994, p. 133) says this:

> A program must encourage, support, and reward the requirements for successful cross-functional teamwork. We must focus the rewards on such things as the coordination of all functions toward the achievement of team goals, the reduction of conflicts among departments, leadership that brings team members together, and results that come from the integration of diverse priorities.

Another way to monitor the progress of teams and individuals is to create performance measurements that encourage the improvement of teams. In *Beyond Corporate Transformation*, Christopher Head (1997, p.170) states some important things an organization can do to develop new and effective performance measures:

Under the new performance measurement system, companies have their newly established "natural" work teams gather the feedback required to help them continually improve their performance. The new measurement system also empowers teams to measure, manage, and improve their piece of the process. An organization can develop a new system by incorporating the following five principles:

1. Let teams take the lead in designing the new system
2. Create process measures, not functional measures
3. Use only a few key measurements
4. Make sure that management does not use the new system to punish or control teams
5. Link together a balanced set of long-term and short-term performance and learning measures.

Christopher Head says it is *equally* important that you should not lose sight of the individual. Individuals need ongoing feedback for their own personal development. He says that companies must also create performance-based compensation systems (pp. 183–184):

In newly transformed organizations employees are responsible for managing their performance, improving their work, working with customers, learning new skills, and developing new capabilities. With these new-found responsibilities there must follow a performance-based compensation system that motivates and rewards performance across all of these areas—a compensation system that recognizes, rewards, and retains employees. . . .

The new system should be simple and easy to understand and administer. It should reinforce the goals of the organization and be economically and legally sound. Most importantly, compensation should be linked to individual, team, and company performance. To create this type of systems you should incorporate the following five principles:

1. Use compensation teams to create the new system.
2. Create a proper mix of individual, team, and business unit performance measures.
3. Share results to motivate and reward teams that deliver value to their customers.
4. Place no caps on the teams' bonuses or rewards.
5. Dispense bonuses and/or rewards, and non-monetary accolades, frequently.

Teams should be recognized and rewarded as a group and this act must be timely and specific. There could be a sharing rally, a team presentation to management, a special quality day, or some other form of recognition. Rewards may be monetary or nonmonetary, but they must express the organization's gratitude for a job well done and be valued by the receiving teams. We can learn from the staff of Goodmeasure, Inc. They authored a book (1988) in which they suggest (p. 158) that recognition and rewards are an important part of good managerial practice for several reasons:

- Recognition will help create an environment that motivates your people to commit themselves to your quality or productivity improvement efforts.
- Recognition is a way for your organization to express its acknowledgment of and appreciation of managers and employees who have worked hard and well to further the goals of quality and productivity improvement.
- Recognition is a way for the organization to give something to employees and managers.
- Recognition helps to reinforce a culture of pride and sense of being "winners."
- Recognition helps reinforce teamwork in your organization.
- Recognition bolsters self-esteem.

Finally, one way to value and reward your teams is to help them learn continuously. For teams to succeed, organizations need to be *learning* organizations in which teams and individuals can continuously improve and/or develop new skills. As individuals learn more companies should reward them more. This way you are rewarding teams for performance and learning.

A good way to start is by using the tools in stage eight. These tools are very useful in the preparation and presentation process. Tool 39 is effective in soliciting feedback from customers, process owners, subject matter expects, etc. Tool 40 shows a team's progress, achievement, or action proposal, and you can use it to update management on projects, changes, or potential problem areas.

Stage Eight: Navigator Tools for Team Recognition and Reward

39	(67)	PP	Different Point of View
40	(139)	PP	Presentations

There are five other tools from previous stages that you can also use to reward and recognize teams. Team Meeting Evaluation (tool 7) will give feedback on the effectiveness of team dynamics and the team's problem-solving process. Team Mirror (tool 8) can compare and evaluate team dynamics and performance. Team Process Assessment (tool 9) will rate areas such as problem solving, team dynamics, and administrative procedures. Idea Borrowing (tool 31) will help you select ideas from inside and outside the organization. Wildest Idea Technique (tool 37) uses team recognition and reward as its how-to-use example. All together, these tools should provide you with ample and accurate information to (1) know the purpose, status, and productivity of each team, and (2) effectively reward them.

Some Team Lessons from Geese

I would like to share a few last lessons from an unlikely source. The author of this piece is unknown, but in observing a simple flock of geese, he or she has created a great analogy for team behavior and success:

> *There are some valuable lessons given to us every day if we take the time*
> *to look and observe our world and the creatures around us.*
> *As we begin another year, perhaps the geese can*
> *show us a way to make our world a better place.*

1. As each bird flaps its wings, it creates an uplift for the bird following. By flying in a V formation, the whole flock adds 71 percent more to its flying range than if each bird flew alone.

   Lesson: People who share a common direction and sense of community can get where they are going quicker and easier when they are traveling on the shared power of one another.

2. Whenever a goose falls out of formation, it suddenly feels the drag and resistance of trying to fly alone, and quickly gets back into formation to take advantage of the lifting power of the bird immediately in front.

   Lesson: If we have as much sense as a goose, we will stay in formation with those who are headed where we want to go.

3. When the lead goose gets tired, it rotates back into the formation and another goose flies at the point position.

   Lesson: It pays to take turns doing the hard tasks and sharing the leadership to promote healthy interdependence with one another.

4. In formation, the geese from behind honk to encourage those up front to keep up their speed.

   Lesson: We need to make sure our honking from behind is encouraging, not damaging or defeating.

5. When a goose gets sick, or wounded, or shot down, two geese drop out of formation and follow it down to help and protect it. They stay with it until it is able to fly again or dies. Then they launch out on their own to join another formation or to catch up with the original flock.

   Lesson: If we have as much sense and compassion as geese, we will also stand by one another in times of trouble.

Conclusion

Tools do not solve problems, *people* do. While a team facilitator makes it easier for a team to problem solve, the application of the appropriate tools by a team also facilitates their problem-solving process. From my 30 years of collecting material and notes about tools and techniques, I know that it is highly instrumental to have the right tool when you need it.

Building effective teams is an important ingredient in developing a continuous improvement process for your company. Generating creativity and innovation by linking together employees from various functional departments—creating cross-functional teams—will assure you of an even higher degree of success. And sustaining these teams with policies that reward them will keep your teams dynamic, fresh, and effective. I believe the 40 tools and eight stages in this guide, as well as six sigma, will not only do these things, but will create a healthy and productive environment where everyone is committed to working together toward one common goal—solving problems. For me, it comes back again to what John Parker Stewart observed about the word **team**:

> **T**ogether
> **E**veryone
> **A**chieves
> **M**ore

Stage One

Navigator Tools to Assess
Organizational Readiness

Organization Readiness Chart

AKA **Capability Assessment Chart**

Changing/Implementing (CI)

tool description

The organization readiness chart is used by planning committees or research teams to verify that the organization is ready and capable of implementing a major change effort. The chart requires open communication and analysis in order to be an effective planning tool.

typical application

- To verify an organization's readiness and capability for planned change.
- To identify preliminary tasks that need to be accomplished to ensure success.

problem-solving phase

➡ Select and define problem or opportunity

Identify and analyze causes or potential change

➡ Develop and plan possible solutions or change

Implement and evaluate solution or change

➡ Measure and report solution or change results

Recognize and reward team efforts

links to other tools in *Tool Navigator™*

before

Data collection strategy

Venn diagram

Organization mapping

Two-dimensional survey grid

Markov analysis

after

SWOT analysis

Action plan

Resource requirements matrix

Barriers-and-aids analysis

Problem specification

notes and key points

- The readiness scale is a recommendation only. Teams should adjust thresholds as desired.

step-by-step procedure

STEP 1 The planning committee or research team openly discusses the readiness of the organization. See example *Ready for Self-Directed Work Teams?*

STEP 2 All meeting participants fill in the chart, calculate a total score, and return the chart to the team facilitator.

STEP 3 A flip chart is used to record all total scores and "high concern" scores that may indicate problem areas or opportunities for improvement.

STEP 4 Following the display of scores, additional discussion takes place for the purpose of formulating required action.

STEP 5 Charts are dated and saved for future reference.

example of tool application

Ready for Self-Directed Work Teams?   Date: xx/xx/xx
Mark "0" for No Concern   "2" for Some Concern   "4" for High Concern
1. _____ A supportive climate in the organization
2. _____ Ongoing commitment to total quality management
3. _____ Active employee involvement is evident
4. _____ Employee share in the decision-making process
5. _____ Management's guidance and expectation for teams (at start-up)
6. _____ Supervisory staff's attitude toward teaming
7. _____ Rewards and recognition for teams
8. _____ Resource commitment (financial, facilities, equipment)
9. _____ Organizational constraints (personnel, budget, priorities)
10. _____ Consultation and evaluation support is available
11. _____ Communication channels (interfacing, reporting, feedback)
12. _____ Training of team members (team dynamics, problem-solving tools)
13. _____ Commitment to team meeting schedules and action items
14. _____ Availability of administrative forms and procedures (for teams)
15. _____ Other_____
_____ Total Score
Readiness Scale: 0–15 = *ready to start;* 16–30 = *more preparation required;* 31+ = *lack of readiness*

Navigator Tools for Team Building and Effectiveness

Circles of Influence

2

Team Building (TB)

tool description

The circles of influence tool allows a team to verify the extent of its self-management, decision-making authority, and problem-solving capability. Circles are used to display forces or problems that are within the team's influence or that are outside the team's influence.

typical application

- To evaluate problems and forces influencing a team's performance.
- To identify a team's areas of responsibility and influence.
- To verify team management and authority.
- To empower a team by increasing its influence and defining accountability.

problem-solving phase

Select and define problem or opportunity

Identify and analyze causes or potential change

➡ Develop and plan possible solutions or change

➡ Implement and evaluate solution or change

➡ Measure and report solution or change results

Recognize and reward team efforts

links to other tools in *Tool Navigator*™

before

Brainstorming

Consensus decision making

Team process assessment

Buzz group

Team mirror

after

Relationship map

Sociogram

Delphi method

Critical dialogue

Multivoting

notes and key points

- Each participant takes no more than 10 minutes to list problems for consideration.
- Use coding such as A-1, B-1, C-1, etc., to designate problems placed into circles of influence A-B-C.

step-by-step procedure

STEP 1   The team's facilitator draws three circles of influence on a flip chart and explains the purpose and application of this tool. A team discussion follows.

STEP 2   The facilitator starts the team by providing an example problem for each circle of influence. Further clarification takes place to ensure that each participant understands the process.

STEP 3   Participants are asked to develop a list of existing and perceived problems that affect the team's present performance.

STEP 4   Once participants have completed their lists, the facilitator collects these lists for encoding and charting problems. See example *A Team's Problem-Solving Ability*.

STEP 5   All listed problems are discussed and consensus is reached on where problems should be charted: circle A, B, or C. The first problem determined to be in circle A should be encoded as A-1.

STEP 6   All charted problems are recorded on flip charts titled *Circle A*, *Circle B*, and *Circle C*, as shown in the example. A discussion follows on the team's ability to control or influence problems.

STEP 7   Finally, the team explores ways to increase the team's influence, expand on its area of responsibility, and, therefore, improve team performance.

example of tool application

A Team's Problem-Solving Ability

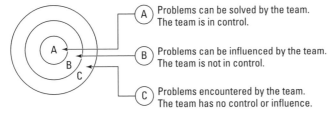

A — Problems can be solved by the team.
The team is in control.

B — Problems can be influenced by the team.
The team is not in control.

C — Problems encountered by the team.
The team has no control or influence.

Date: xx/xx/xx

Circle A	Circle B	Circle C
A-1 Membership	B-1 Inter-group participation	C-1 Customer contacts
A-2 Work assignments	B-2 Rules	C-2 Work ethic
A-3 Safety	B-3 Schedule	C-3 Policy
A-4 Performance	B-4 Reports	C-4 Regulatory
A-5 Communications	B-5 Resources	C-5 Compensation
A-6 Cooperation	B-6 Turnover	C-6 Contracts
A-7 Relationships		

Fishbowls

tool description

Fishbowls are very structured and facilitated discussions on some problem or issue by half of the team's participants while the other half of the team observes the process. After a predetermined time period, both halves switch roles. Fishbowls are ideal for team dynamics to serve as team training, as well as to explore in-depth an issue or problem.

typical application

- To train teams to communicate effectively, have discussions among equals, and promote an open sharing of ideas.
- To keep participants focused on an issue or problem.
- To start a problem-solving effort.
- To observe and analyze team dynamics.

problem-solving phase

➡ Select and define problem or opportunity

➡ Identify and analyze causes or potential change

➡ Develop and plan possible solutions or change

Implement and evaluate solution or change

Measure and report solution or change results

Recognize and reward team efforts

links to other tools in *Tool Navigator*™

before

Sociogram

Buzz group

Observation

Circle response

Circles of influence

after

Rotating roles

Different point of view

Consensus decision making

Critical dialogue

Presentation

notes and key points

- Ensure that participants switch roles only as directed.
- Each participant's input is limited to 1 minute per input.
- Total time for the fishbowl activity is 60 minutes.

step-by-step procedure

STEP 1   The facilitator provides an overview of the fishbowl process. Participants draw numbers and are divided into odd and even numbers. At the beginning, the odd-numbered participants are seated in the inner circle, the fishbowl. Even-numbered participants take a seat in the outer circle.

STEP 2   Next, the facilitator displays the issue to be discussed, informs the inner ring when the discussion starts and that they have 30 minutes to discuss the issue. A moderator is selected and receives a prepared set of questions to keep the discussion stimulating and challenging. Participants are asked to keep their input to 1 minute per issue. The moderator takes notes on the discussion for team sharing. See example *How Do We Change the Culture in an Organization?*

STEP 3   The participants of the outer ring are assigned roles as observers. Their silent note taking will capture data on conflict, interruptions, drifting to other issues, dominant or less expressive participants, and other situations.

STEP 4   The facilitator starts the clock and the discussion and observations take place. After 30 minutes, the fishbowl is stopped and the observers provide feedback on their observations.

STEP 5   Roles are switched and the outer ring participants (even numbers) move to the inner ring. Steps 2 through 4 above are repeated to complete the fishbowl.

STEP 6   Both moderators share their discussion notes and a joint discussion may now take place on the issue, as shown in the example.

example of tool application

**How Do We Change the Culture
in an Organization?**

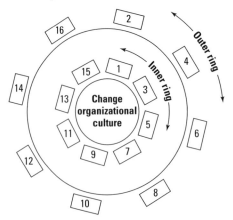

Fishbowl Observations	Date: xx/xx/xx

Team Dynamics
 – Some dominant individuals

 – Some participants struggled

 – Timing was frustrating to some

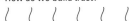

Discussion items
 – Involve people in any change

 – Teach learning organization concepts

 – How do we build trust?

Organization Mapping

tool description

The organization mapping technique examines the team's relationships with other teams or business units within the organization. A map illustrates communication links and the frequency and importance of interactions. Recorded notes suggest improvement areas.

typical application

- To illustrate and define a team's relationships within an organization.
- To map ongoing interactions and to search for ways to improve those interactions.

problem-solving phase

➡ Select and define problem or opportunity
➡ Identify and analyze causes or potential change
  Develop and plan possible solutions or change
  Implement and evaluate solution or change
  Measure and report solution or change results
  Recognize and reward team efforts

links to other tools in *Tool Navigator*™

before

Circle response
Sociogram
Buzz group
Observation
Consensus decision making

after

Relationship map
Deployment chart (down-across)
Run-it-by
Team mirror
Presentation

notes and key points

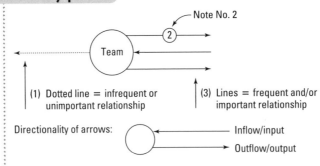

step-by-step procedure

STEP 1   The team facilitator explains the purpose and application of this tool. A circle is drawn in the center of a whiteboard to start the organization mapping process.

STEP 2   Participants identify linkages and relationships with other teams or business units and establish the frequency and importance of these relationships. See example *Reproduction Team Services*.

STEP 3   Systematically, a map is drawn that displays links, partnerships, frequency and importance of relationships, and contact identification.

STEP 4   The participants engage in a discussion that explores improvements in the current network and problems that need to be resolved.

STEP 5   Notes are added to the organization map, a final check is performed so that the map reflects the current status, and finally, the map is dated.

example of tool application

Reproduction Team Services

Date: xx/xx/xx

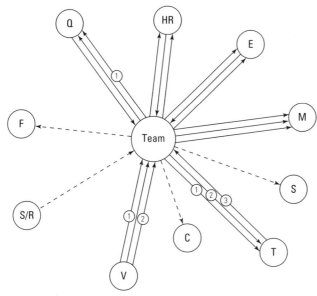

Interactions
HR – Human Resources
E – Engineering
M – Manufacturing
S – Sales
T – Training
C – Consultants
V – Vendors
S/R – Shipping/receiving
F – Finance
Q – Quality

Notes: Q–1: *Let's invite quality section to assist us in our*
              quality improvement efforts
        V–1: *Negotiate faster turnaround times*
        V–2: *Return damaged stock*
        T–1: *Need longer time frames to print*
        T–2: *Updating of course masters required*
        T–3: *We need to be more responsive to customers*

Relationship Map

5

AKA **N/A**

Team Building (TB)

tool description

The relationship map directs the emphasis on people and their interactions among teams from different functional units. It helps a team visualize the process steps and brainstorm some process-improvement ideas. The map also fosters a common understanding of the overall process.

typical application

- To show relationship and interactions of teams working together to reach a common goal.
- To map out process steps for the purpose of surfacing process-improvement opportunities.

problem-solving phase

➡ Select and define problem or opportunity

➡ Identify and analyze causes or potential change

➡ Develop and plan possible solutions or change

Implement and evaluate solution or change

Measure and report solution or change results

Recognize and reward team efforts

links to other tools in *Tool Navigator*™

before

Organization mapping

Sociogram

Circle response

Observation

Circles of influence

after

Process mapping

Deployment chart (down-across)

Process analysis

Different point of view

Potential problem analysis (PPA)

notes and key points

Similar to a process map, a relationship map uses some basic symbols:

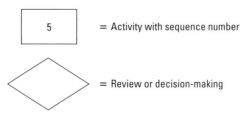

= Activity with sequence number

= Review or decision-making

step-by-step procedure

STEP 1 The team facilitator reviews, with the participants, the steps for constructing a relationship map.

STEP 2 Next, all teams or functional units that are involved in the process are listed on a whiteboard. See example *Preliminary Analysis: ISO-9000 Implementation*.

STEP 3 Process steps are identified and sequenced in order of completion.

STEP 4 The relationship map is completed by fully connecting all process activities following the sequence steps as shown in the example.

STEP 5 Notes are added to fully explain what the relationships are and what is being accomplished.

STEP 6 Finally, the map is dated and distributed to all interested parties.

example of tool application

Preliminary Analysis: ISO-9000 Implementation

Date: xx/xx/xx

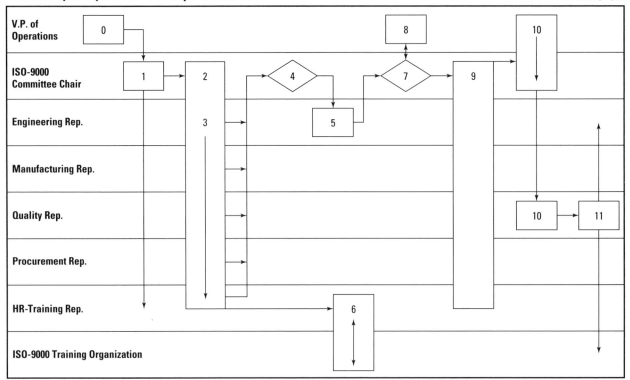

Process Sequence Steps:

0. V.P. of Operations appoints ISO-9000 chair.

1. Company ISO-9000 review committee established.

2. Company representatives attend orientation meeting.

3. Research tasks assigned
   - Engineering
   - Manufacturing
   - Quality
   - Procurement
   - HR (training)
   - Proposal development
   - Data collection requirements
   - Quality manual development
   - Supplier involvement
   - Training requirements

4. Researched information reviewed.

5. Engineering compiles proposal information.

6. Training contacts outside ISO-9000 source.

7. Proposal draft reviewed and forwarded to operations.

8. Next step authorization received.

9. Representatives prepare budgets for their respective units.

10. Quality department appointed leadership role.

11. First ISO-9000 implementation committee meeting scheduled.

Sociogram

AKA **Interaction Diagram, Sociometric Diagram**

Team Building (TB)

tool description

The sociogram is an interaction diagram that illustrates intrateam communication patterns, interpersonal dynamics, and compatibility among team participants. Introduced by J. L. Moreno in 1934, the sociogram is helpful in promoting partnerships, team cohesiveness, and mutual acceptance; it therefore allows more participation and openness in teams.

typical application

- To diagram a team's interpersonal relationships and cooperation.
- To obtain an understanding of intrateam interactions and acceptance of team participants.

problem-solving phase

Select and define problem or opportunity
➡ Identify and analyze causes or potential change
➡ Develop and plan possible solutions or change
Implement and evaluate solution or change
Measure and report solution or change results
Recognize and reward team efforts

**links to
other tools in
Tool Navigator™**

before
Demographic analysis
Circles of influence
Audience analysis
Organization mapping
Observation

after
Critical dialogue
Relationship map
Rotating roles
Pair matching overlay
Resource histogram

- Sociogram legend:

Selector ——————▶ Selected
Rejecter ———//——▶ Rejected
Mutual ◀——————▶ Choice (or acceptance)

- A variation of showing interactions is to draw the number of choices (mentions) given or received:

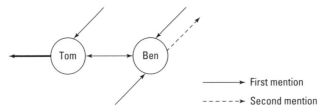

——————▶ First mention
- - - - -▶ Second mention

- Limit to 10 the number of people in a sociogram.

step-by-step procedure

STEP 1　Periodically, the team facilitator, coach, or a designated team partici-pant performs observations of team behavior and interpersonal communications.

STEP 2　Notes on communication patterns, acceptance, and rejection, "who inter-acts with whom" (Moreno), and amount of participation are collected.

STEP 3　Next, a sociogram is drawn and shared with the team. An open discus-sion follows on ways to improve the team's performance.

STEP 4　A list of possible improvements is developed.

example of tool application

Team Interpersonal Dynamics

Date: xx/xx/xx

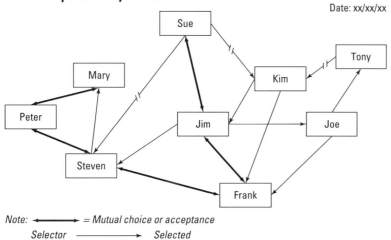

Note: ◄──────► = Mutual choice or acceptance
      Selector ──────► Selected
      Rejecter ───//──► Rejected

Team Meeting Evaluation

7

Team Building (TB)

tool description

The team meeting evaluation surveys provide timely feedback on the effectiveness of the problem-solving process, team dynamics, and the administrative procedures used to ensure that the team stays focused and is moving toward its goals.

typical application

- To evaluate a team's process and progress.
- To periodically monitor the effectiveness of team meetings.
- To search for areas of improvements.

problem-solving phase

Select and define problem or opportunity
➡ Identify and analyze causes or potential change
Develop and plan possible solutions or change
Implement and evaluate solution or change
➡ Measure and report solution or change results
➡ Recognize and reward team efforts

links to other tools in *Tool Navigator*™

before
Circle response
Buzz group
Surveying
Relationship map
Interview technique

after
Rotating roles
Team process assessment
Sociogram
Different point of view
Critical dialog

notes and key points

- Participants' completed meeting evaluation forms should be summarized after each meeting and process/progress results fed back to the team. Use the team process assessment tool for this purpose.
- The use of Likert scale designations (very satisfactory to very unsatisfactory, strongly agree to strongly disagree, etc.) is best determined by the team.

step-by-step procedure

STEP 1   After every team meeting, or periodically if the team decides it, participants fill out the team evaluation survey form.

STEP 2   The team leader or team facilitator summarizes all responses and compares the results with those of the previous meeting. Of particular interest may be the rating averages and any patterns or variations from the expected results.

STEP 3   The rating results and suggestions made are discussed at the beginning of the next scheduled team meeting.

STEP 4   All completed forms should be dated and saved for pattern analysis.

example of tool application

Team Meeting Feedback

Team: Mfg.–No. 1	Meeting Evaluation No. 3				Date xx/xx/xx

Please evaluate this meeting by circling your choice
5 = Very satisfactory; 4 = Satisfactory; 3 = Average; 2 = Unsatisfactory; 1 = Very unsatisfactory

Your observation/perception

1. The team meeting started/ended on time	(5)	4	3	2	1
2. The agenda was displayed and followed	(5)	4	3	2	1
3. Team members understood meeting's purpose	5	(4)	3	2	1
4. The team's action log was reviewed	5	(4)	3	2	1
5. All team members participated	5	4	(3)	2	1
6. The facilitator kept meeting on topic	5	(4)	3	2	1
7. Team communications were open and supportive	5	(4)	3	2	1
8. The team managed time efficiently	(5)	4	3	2	1
9. Good progress was made during this meeting	(5)	4	3	2	1
10. Team used appropriate decision-making methods	5	(4)	3	2	1
11. Next step action items were assigned	(5)	4	3	2	1
12. The facilitator summarized results	(5)	4	3	2	1

Any suggestions? _____

	5s	4s	3s	2s	1s
Thank You					
Total circled	6	5	1	0	0
Total score:	53				
File: Team–Mfg.–No. 1 **Average rating:**	4.42				

Team Mirror

Team Building (TB)

tool description

The team mirror technique is used to compare and evaluate team dynamics and performance. It allows teams to view each other and perform a mutual analysis of team effectiveness. All observations are shared for the purpose of furthering team development.

typical application

- To allow teams to share perceptions and suggest ways for improved cooperation among teams.
- To train teams.
- To improve team effectiveness.

problem-solving phase

Select and define problem or opportunity

Identify and analyze causes or potential change

➡ Develop and plan possible solutions or change

Implement and evaluate solution or change

Measure and report solution or change results

➡ Recognize and reward team efforts

---

links to other tools in *Tool Navigator*™

before
Consensus decision making
Sociogram
Influence diagram
Circle response
Buzz group

after
Team meeting evaluation
Rotating roles
Team process assessment
Different point of view
Fishbowls

notes and key points

- This analysis requires one large and one small room for joint and separate team meetings.

step-by-step procedure

STEP 1 Teams agree to mutually analyze their effectiveness and engage an outside facilitator.

STEP 2 The facilitator reviews the team mirror process with both teams and displays a few questions on a flip chart. Both teams are asked to respond to:
- How are we doing?
- How are they doing?
- How do they think we are doing?
- How can we improve?
- How can they improve?
- How can we work together to improve?

STEP 3 One of the teams is asked to move to a separate room (or both teams if two rooms are available) so they can discuss and record their responses. See example *Team Effectiveness Training.*

STEP 4 After approximately 30 minutes both teams rejoin and exchange responses.

STEP 5 Next, the facilitator leads a discussion on improvement opportunities and the teams reach consensus on what changes can be made to increase the effectiveness of both teams.

example of tool application

Team Effectiveness Training

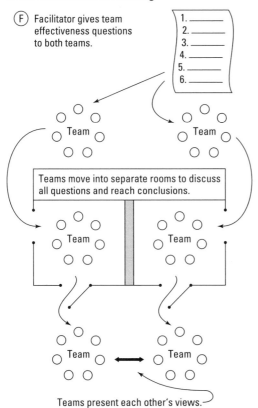

(F) Facilitator gives team
    effectiveness questions
    to both teams.

1. _____
2. _____
3. _____
4. _____
5. _____
6. _____

Team

Team

Teams move into separate rooms to discuss
all questions and reach conclusions.

Team

Team

Team

Team

Teams present each other's views.

(F) Facilitator leads discussion, teams share ideas and
    reach consensus on changes to be made to improve
    team interactions and effectiveness.

Team Process Assessment

AKA **N/A**

Team Building (TB)

tool description

The team process assessment technique verifies team performance using a Likert rating scale. Areas of interest such as problem-solving activities, team dynamics, and administrative procedures are rated, and results are fed back to the team for the purpose of continuous improvement.

typical application

- To rate a team's process and progress.
- To monitor the effectiveness of team meetings.
- To provide performance feedback.

problem-solving phase

- ➥ Select and define problem or opportunity
- ➥ Identify and analyze causes or potential change
- ➥ Develop and plan possible solutions or change
- Implement and evaluate solution or change
- Measure and report solution or change results
- ➥ Recognize and reward team efforts

notes and key points

- Rating averages used:

  $\bar{X}$ = item average (sum of item ratings ÷ 8)

  $\bar{\bar{X}}$ = overall team average
  (sum of all item ratings ÷ 96)

- Rating scale used:
  - 5 = Very satisfactory
  - 4 = Satisfactory
  - 3 = Average
  - 2 = Unsatisfactory
  - 1 = Very unsatisfactory

---

links to other tools in Tool Navigator™

before

Team meeting evaluation

Surveying

Questionnaires

Interview technique

Gap analysis

after

Rotating roles

Different point of view

Run-it-by

Critical dialogue

What-if-analysis

---

step-by-step procedure

STEP 1 The team leader or facilitator collects all completed team meeting evalua-tions from the participants. See example *Team Mfg.—No. 1 Assessment*.

STEP 2 Next, all responses are summarized and results are compared to those of the previous analysis. Of particular interest may be the rating averages and any patterns or variations from the expected results.

STEP 3 The rating results and suggestions made by participants are discussed at the beginning of the next scheduled team meeting.

STEP 4 All completed forms are dated and saved for pattern analysis.

example of tool application

Team: Mfg.– No. 1 Assessment

Team: *Mfg.–No. 1* **Meeting Evaluation No. 3**										Date *xx/xx/xx*
Participants' Observations/Perceptions	**Participant Responses**									**($\bar{X}$)**
1. The team meeting started/ended on time	5	4	5	4	3	4	4	5	—	—	4.25
2. The agenda was displayed and followed	5	3	4	4	5	5	4	5	—	—	4.38
3. Team members understood meeting's purpose	4	4	3	5	3	3	4	5	—	—	3.88
4. The team's action log was reviewed	4	5	4	5	5	5	5	5	—	—	4.75
5. All team members participated	3	2	3	2	3	1	4	3	—	—	2.63
6. The facilitator kept meeting on topic	4	5	4	3	5	5	5	4	—	—	4.38
7. Team communications were open and supportive	4	4	4	5	3	4	5	3	—	—	4.00
8. The team managed time efficiently	5	4	5	4	4	3	3	5	—	—	4.13
9. Good progress was made during this meeting	5	5	4	3	4	3	4	5	—	—	4.13
10. Team used appropriate decision-making methods	4	4	3	1	2	3	5	4	—	—	3.25
11. Next step action items were assigned	5	3	4	3	4	3	5	4	—	—	3.88
12. The facilitator summarized results	5	4	4	4	5	5	5	4	—	—	4.50
File: Team–Mfg.–No. 1							**Overall team average $\bar{\bar{X}}$ = 3.95**			

Notes: 1. See Team Meeting Evaluation Survey
   2. Rating responses: 5 = very satisfactory; 4 = satisfactory; 3 = average; 2 = unsatisfactory; 1 = very unsatisfactory

Navigator Tools for Team Member Assignment

Responsibility Matrix

AKA **Accountability Grid**

Changing/Implementing (CI)

tool description

A responsibility matrix is used to identify decisions to be made, major activities to be completed, and persons or groups involved in a change project. Project management requires constant tracking of activities and schedule; a responsibility matrix provides the assignments and understanding of employees' roles and resources required to complete a project.

typical application

- To display decision requirements, activities to be completed, and key personnel involved in a project management setting.
- To provide a common understanding of a project's people and resource requirements and allocation.

problem-solving phase

Select and define problem or opportunity
Identify and analyze causes or potential change
➡ Develop and plan possible solutions or change
➡ Implement and evaluate solution or change
Measure and report solution or change results
Recognize and reward team efforts

links to other tools in *Tool Navigator*™

before

Problem analysis

Checklist

Demographic analysis

Circle response

Consensus decision making

after

Resource histogram

Action plan

Basili data collection method

Project planning log

Milestones chart

notes and key points

- No cell may contain more than one role.
- Avoid splitting primary responsibility (R) for action.
- Avoid assigning too many approvals (A) to any one item.
- Coding: Typical codes have been assigned in this example. Additional designations may be needed.

step-by-step procedure

STEP 1   A facilitated planning team or committee identifies major project activities and responsibilities.

STEP 2   The facilitator creates a responsibility matrix on a whiteboard and requests participants' assistance in completing the matrix. Activities and actors are listed. See example *Establishment of Continuous Improvement Teams*.

STEP 3   Next, participants determine personnel assignments and respective roles in the completion of project activities. A coding scheme is used as shown in this example.

STEP 4   Finally, the completed responsibility matrix is checked, revised, and dated.

example of tool application

Establishment of Continuous Improvement Teams   Date xx/xx/xx

Decisions or Activities	Person or Team									
	HR Director	OPS Manager	Team Leader	Team Facilitator	Team Members	Budget Admin.	Shift A Supervisor	Shift B Supervisor	Quality Director	VP of OPS
Member recruitment	S	A	R	—	I	S	I	I	I	C
Schedule/facilities	I	A	R	S	I	S	C	C	I	—
Administrative support	S	S	R	—	I	A	I	I	C	—
Role assignments	—	A	R	C	I	—	—	—	—	—
Team guidelines	R	S	S	C	I	—	I	I	A	—
Team training	R	A	—	S	I	S	I	I	C	—
Recognition rewards	R	S	I	I	I	S	I	I	C	A

Codes: A = Approval role   B = Responsibility for action   S = Support role;
       C = Consultation role   I = Information/notification role   — = Irrelevant

Rotating Roles

tool description

The rotating roles activity is a very effective tool for expanding a team's perspectives on the possible consequences or problems resulting from organizational change or from implementation efforts for process, product, or service improvements. Rotating between roles allows participants to bring forward different views in that role or position as a process owner or stakeholder, views that often do not surface unless you "act out" a particular role.

typical application

- To collect more perspectives or views on the problem at hand.
- To identify the concerns, issues, or opportunities for a team's consideration before taking action.
- To see different possibilities by "acting out" a particular process owner's role or position in the organization.

problem-solving phase

Select and define problem or opportunity

➡ Identify and analyze causes or potential change

➡ Develop and plan possible solutions or change

Implement and evaluate solution or change

Measure and report solution or change results

Recognize and reward team efforts

links to other tools in *Tool Navigator*™

before

Different point of view

Circles of influence

Fishbowls

Customer acquisition/defection matrix

Interview technique

after

Presentation

Critical dialogue

Team meeting evaluation

Starbursting

What-if-analysis

notes and key points

- Works best with 5–8 participants.
- Have one prepared flip chart for each role.
- Rotate one space at a time until all participants have had each role.
- No "pass" is permitted!

step-by-step procedure

STEP 1 The facilitator prepares a wheel with participants' names and writes the problem in the center of the wheel. Role cards and a flip chart for each role must also be prepared. See example *Potential Problems with the Establishment of Flextime.*

STEP 2 Participants are seated around the table and the facilitator explains the purpose and rules of the activity.

STEP 3 Every participant views the problem from his/her present role and records concerns, insights, ideas, or recommendations on the appropriate flip chart prepared for this role. After everyone has finished, the wheel is rotated one position or, as an option, participants move to the next chair.

STEP 4 This process of rotation continues, and ideas are recorded on the flip charts, until all participants have rotated through all roles. No "pass" is allowed.

STEP 5 The facilitator ends the session and compiles flip chart information for the team's next step in the problem solving or quality improvement effort as shown in the example.

example of tool application

Potential Problems with the Establishment of Flextime

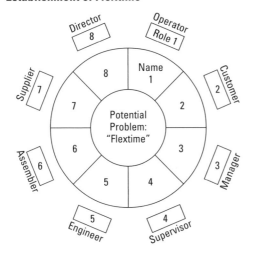

Points of view	Date: xx/xx/xx
– Difficult timekeeping procedures	
– Less absenteeism (single parents)	
– Quality of work life	
– Customer cannot reach employee	
– Effective communications during core hours	

– Scheduling problems (staff meetings, etc.)
– Performance observation/appraisal

Stage Four

Navigator Tools for
First Team Activities

Problem Specification

12

Planning/Presenting (PP)

tool description

The problem specification tool provides team members with a shared understanding of a problem. Moreover it points to an orderly first step of collecting specific, appropriate data for the purpose of writing a problem statement that clearly defines the unacceptable "as is" situation, any process variance, or its potential causes. The problem specification should also describe the "should be" state of the situation or process to be improved.

typical application

- To establish a problem-solving goal or improvement target.
- To clarify a vague condition perceived as a problem.
- To collect data relevant to the problem and possibly indicative of the root causes.
- To satisfy the need for more data.

problem-solving phase

➥ Select and define problem or opportunity
➥ Identify and analyze causes or potential change
   Develop and plan possible solutions or change
   Implement and evaluate solution or change
   Measure and report solution or change results
   Recognize and reward team efforts

links to other tools in *Tool Navigator*™

before

Data collection strategy
Interview technique
Multivariable chart
Cause and effect diagram (CED)
Pareto chart

after

What-if analysis
Process mapping
Work flow analysis (WFA)
Process analysis
Systems analysis diagram

notes and key points

- A superior problem specification reflects measurable data: Quantitatively expressed data are numbers, percentages, frequencies, time periods, amounts, rate durations, etc. Qualitatively expressed data are perceptions, demographics, or any nominal data scales.

step-by-step procedure

STEP 1   The team starts the problem specifiction process by discussing the current situation; this situation is called the *as is* on the problem specification form. Expand the information to include all recorded data and verbal input. See example *Problem Specification—Quality of Service*.

STEP 2   Next, the preferred situation, called *should be* on the form, is discussed. This ideal state reflects a perceived gap in process performance from the *as is* state.

STEP 3   Close the performance gap between the two states by filling in the information as illustrated by numbers 1 and 2 on the example problem specification form.

STEP 4   Using the information compiled in 1 and 2 on the example, complete the form by providing the appropriate information for the two columns: *problem occurs* 3 and *problem is resolved* 4 .

In the final step, develop a final problem statement that encompasses the critical elements of the problem as developed on the form.

STEP 5   The team finalizes the problem statement shown as 5 on the form; team consensus is reached, and the entire team signs off on it.

example of tool application

Quality of Service

Problem Specification—Quality of Service	Date xx/xx/xx

❶ As is situation/condition
Service cycle time is 12 days, the customer satisfaction index rating is low, and recalls average 7 per month.

❷ Should be target/goal
Cycle time = 8.5 days, CSI rating = high, and recalls average 3 per month (per benchmark data)

When

❸ Problem occurs
– At the end of the month (last six months)
– Missed service calls

❹ Problem is resolved
– Balanced scheduling
– More training
– Concerns for quality

Where

– All service areas
– Business districts

– Timely service regardless of service area

Impact

– 15% increase in customer complaints

– Less than 2% recalls on service calls

People/Groups

– Service department technicians

– Service department technicians provide better quality service

Related Information

– Pareto analysis and customer satisfaction survey results are available

❺ Final problem statement
The previous six months' service calls schedule produced a 15% increase of customer complaints. Causes appear to be lengthy cycle time (delays) and quality of service (recalls).

Process Mapping

AKA **Cross-Functional Process Map**

Team Building (TB)

tool description

The process mapping tool is of great value for teams in documenting the existing process. It identifies and maps all cross-functional processes, process owners (organizations), metrics, and estimated processing time or mapped activities. A finalized process map ensures a thorough understanding of the "as is" process and provides baseline input data for a process improvement team.

typical application

- To mark a visual map of the process in order to perform the analysis necessary for identifying problematic conditions.
- To identify, map, analyze, and prepare *as is* and *should be* process maps.
- To draw a map for process understanding and to discover potential areas for improvement.
- To reduce cycle time of mapped activities.

problem-solving phase

➥ Select and define problem or opportunity

➥ Identify and analyze causes or potential change

Develop and plan possible solutions or change

Implement and evaluate solution or change

Measure and report solution or change results

Recognize and reward team efforts

links to other tools in *Tool Navigator™*

before

Affinity diagram

Systems analysis diagram

Pareto chart

Potential problem analysis (PPA)

Needs analysis

after

Cycle time flowchart

Gap analysis

Force field analysis (FFA)

Barriers-and-aids analysis

Activity analysis

notes and key points

- Symbols and scale:

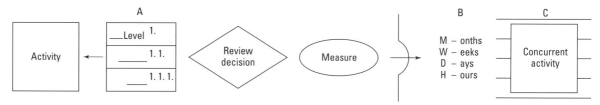

A – Optional level of detail for activities
B – Time scale: Months (M), Weeks (W), Days (D), Hours (H).
C – Four organizations performing activity concurrently

- "Connectors" example:

- A process map can be developed at the macro, mini, or micro level of an organizational process.

step-by-step procedure

STEP 1   A team facilitator assembles a team of cross-functional representatives to assist the development of the process map.

STEP 2   The team decides on the level of detail to be mapped—that is macro (overview), mini (most activities), and micro (very detailed, specific tasks).

STEP 3   Next, the process start and stop points are determined.

STEP 4   As a prerequisite activity, four flip charts are prepared to serve as input data to the process-mapping procedure:

   – A listing of all organizations or work groups. Sequence list in order of occurrence.

   – A listing of all major functions or activities. Sequence list in order of occurrence.

   – A listing of all reviews, audits, approvals, or other decision-making activities. Sequence list in order of occurrence.

step-by-step procedure (continued)

– A listing of all measurements (metrics) in the following categories: process, results, resources, and customer satisfaction. Sequence list in order of occurrence.

STEP 5   The team facilitator, on a whiteboard, draws the process map as directed and checked by the team. The listings of process sequences "organizations," "major functions," "decision-making," and "metrics" are referenced, in order of occurrence, to map out the complete process. See example *Process: Prepare Draft of Action Plans*.

STEP 6   Finally, the team checks the completed map, final revisions are made, and the map is titled and dated. The facilitator redraws the process map on flip charts for future reference.

Process Selection Matrix

14

Changing/Implementing (CI)

tool description

A process selection matrix uses a set of criteria for prioritization to determine a team's first choice. Typically, the team establishes the criteria and rating method. Team consensus is the basis for completing the matrix.

typical application

- To prioritize processes, projects, or systems to be used in a problem-solving or major organizational change effort.
- To identify a process or tool that promises the greatest return on total investment.
- To determine ways to improve the organization.

problem-solving phase

Select and define problem or opportunity

Identify and analyze causes or potential change

➡ Develop and plan possible solutions or change

➡ Implement and evaluate solution or change

Measure and report solution or change results

Recognize and reward team efforts

notes and key points

- If two total scores are tied, add both ranks and divide to assign median to both rank positions. Example: Two scores = 19 for rank position (2) and (3), therefore 2 + 3 = 5/2 = 2.5. Rank 2.5 is assigned to both positions, as shown in the example.

links to other tools in *Tool Navigator*™

before

Cost-benefit analysis

Benchmarking

Consensus decision making

Process analysis

Potential problem analysis (PPA)

after

Activity cost matrix

Action plan

Information needs analysis

Decision process flowchart

Basili data collection method

step-by-step procedure

STEP 1   The team facilitator prepares a selection matrix and lists all previously determined processes. See example *Organizational Change—Process Selection.*

STEP 2   Participants brainstorm a set of criteria to be used in the rating process.

STEP 3   Next, participants rate each process on a scale of *high, medium, low* using the consensus decision-making technique.

STEP 4   The facilitator records each rating and totals all rows.

STEP 5   Finally, the process selection matrix is dated and Rank 1 (best choice) is circled.

example of tool application

Organizational Change—Process Selection

Date: xx/xx/xx Process Selection	Customer Impact	Implementation Feasibility	Employee Motivation	Organization's Competitiveness	Return on Investment	Total	Rank
Just-in-time (JIT) manufacturing	H	L	M	M	H	17	4.5
Integrated product development	H	H	H	H	M	23	(1)
Self-managed work teams	M	H	H	M	M	19	2.5
Hoshin planning system	L	M	L	L	L	7	6
ISO-9000 quality system	H	M	M	H	M	19	2.5
Business process reengineering	M	L	H	H	M	17	4.5

Notes: High = 5, medium = 3, low = 1
Ranking: Highest total is best choice, rank ①

Navigator Tools for Team Consensus and Synergy

Affinity Diagram

AKA **K-J Method, Affinity Analysis**

Team Building (TB)

tool description

First developed and used in the 1960s by Jiro Kawakita, the affinity diagram is the product of a team's brainstorming and consensus activities. This creative process gathers large amounts of data (ideas, issues, opinions, facts, etc.) and organizes them into logical groupings based on the natural relationships among items.

typical application

- Sort by affinity large volume of data.
- Identify key ideas for process improvement.
- Push for creativity and breakthroughs.
- Determine requirements for action plans.
- Point to potential solutions to problems.
- Identify patterns among seemingly unrelated factors.

problem-solving phase

➡ Select and define problem or opportunity
➡ Identify and analyze causes or potential change
➡ Develop and plan possible solutions or change
   Implement and evaluate solution or change
   Measure and report solution or change results
   Recognize and reward team efforts

links to other tools in *Tool Navigator™*

before

Brainstorming

Brainwriting pool

Events log

Focus group

Consensus decision making

after

Interrelationship digraph (I.D)

Tree diagram

Action plan

Factor analysis

Potential problem analysis (PPA)

notes and key points

- Typical affinity: 6–8 participants, 6–10 groupings of ideas, 50–100 ideas. Connect interrelated groupings with ↔ and cause and effect with →.

step-by-step procedure

STEP 1   Form a diverse team of 6–8 participants.

STEP 2   Write the issue or problem on a flip chart—no further explanation should be given. See example *Improvement of Employee Training*.

STEP 3   Participants generate and record ideas on 3 × 5 cards or post-its, one idea per card.

STEP 4   After approximately 15 minutes, cards are collected and randomly spread out on a large table or posted on a wall.

STEP 5   Participants sort cards in silence, placing related ideas into a grouping. Cards that do not fit are "loners" and kept outside the groups. Groups are reviewed and consensus is reached on ideas that are placed in a particular group.

STEP 6   A search takes place to select a card in each grouping that captures the meaning of that group. This card is considered to be the header and is placed on top of the group. If unable to do this step, a header card is created by the team.

STEP 7   Steps 3–6 are repeated to expand groupings, create others, and gain more ideas.

STEP 8   An affinity diagram is created by laying out groups. Place closely related groups together. Draw outlines for each group with the header card placed on top.

STEP 9   Team checks the final affinity diagram, makes modifications if needed, then titles and dates the diagram.

example of tool application

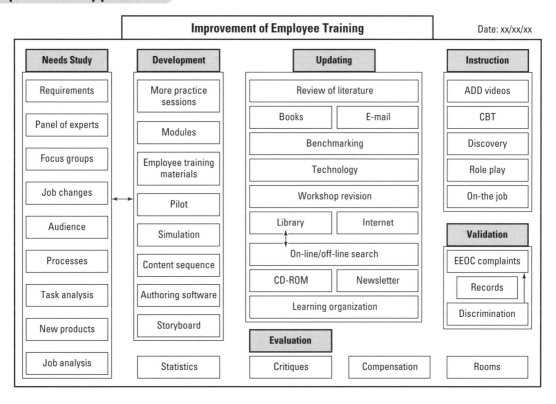

Buzz Group

16

AKA **Buzzing**

Team Building (TB)

tool description

The buzz group technique is of great assistance to team facilitators or presenters when there is a lack of participation or intra-group communication and more involvement is desired. It can be used to initiate discussion on perceived problems, to share experiences and lessons learned, or to achieve team consensus.

typical application

- To explore in detail, and with full participation, process improvement opportunities or ideas for problem resolution.
- To receive each participant's feedback on some issue or experience.
- To involve all persons in the learning process.

problem-solving phase

➡ Select and define problem or opportunity
➡ Identify and analyze causes or potential change
➡ Develop and plan possible solutions or change
Implement and evaluate solution or change
Measure and report solution or change results
➡ Recognize and reward team efforts

notes and key points

- Buzz group size: 4–6 participants.
- Position chairs in a circle so that participants face each other.

links to other tools in *Tool Navigator*™

before
Circle response
Circles of knowledge
Round robin brainstorming
Interview technique
Surveying

after
Consensus decision making
Phillips 66
Critical dialogue
Wildest idea technique
Presentation

96

40 Tools for Cross-Functional Teams

step-by-step procedure

STEP 1 The team facilitator, instructor, or presenter states the purpose for buzzing, asks participants to face one another, and informs all buzz groups that they have approximately eight minutes to "buzz" their topic. Each buzz group selects a spokesperson.

STEP 2 A problem, issue, or idea is displayed to all buzz groups. Groups begin to sort, discuss, or summarize information. See example *Identify Cycle Time Reduction Tools*.

STEP 3 After the allowed time limit, buzz groups are asked to report their findings or ideas.

STEP 4 The facilitator, instructor, or presenter records findings or ideas on flip charts for everyone to see.

STEP 5 Information generated is dated and used on the spot or saved for later reference.

example of tool application

Identify Cycle Time Reduction Tools

Date: xx/xx/xx

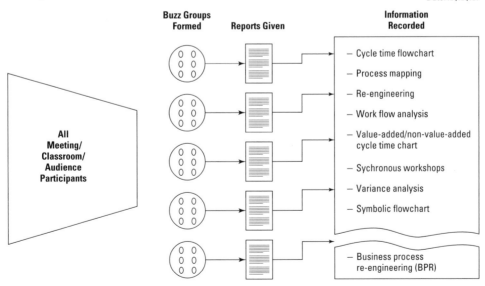

Consensus Decision Making

AKA **Consensus Generator**

Decision Making (DM)

tool description

The consensus decision making tool is an interactive process in which all team participants openly communicate their ideas and reserve feedback and other points of view. The process continues until all team participants are able to accept and support a team decision even though some may not completely agree with it. Reaching consensus often requires greater individual participation, clear communication, and some compromise on well-considered decisions.

typical application

- To reach agreement on a proposed action or next step in a problem-solving effort.
- To gain general agreement and support on a particular idea or issue.
- To allow team participants the opportunity to express and defend their point of view.
- To avoid conflict or rush to a decision.

problem-solving phase

- ➡ Select and define problem or opportunity
- ➡ Identify and analyze causes or potential change
- ➡ Develop and plan possible solutions or change
-    Implement and evaluate solution or change
-    Measure and report solution or change results
- ➡ Recognize and reward team efforts

links to other tools in *Tool Navigator*™

before

Brainstorming

Brainwriting pool

Futures wheel

Affinity diagram

Window analysis

after

Team process assessment

Resource requirements matrix

Objectives matrix (OMAX)

Responsibility matrix

Action plan

notes and key points

- Consensus is reached when:
  - All participants have presented their views.
  - Participants fully understand, accept, and will support the team decision.
  - Even if some participants are not fully satisfied or cannot completely agree with the decision, they do feel that they "can live with it" and will not oppose it.

step-by-step procedure

STEP 1 The team displays a final list of ideas, a proposed problem solution, or process improvement activity. See example *Increase Customer Contact Time for Complaint Handling*.

STEP 2 Team participants clarify all issues, share views, and listen to other ideas or concerns. Ensure that all actively participate in this discussion.

STEP 3 After all information has been shared and alternatives considered, the team develops general agreement with care being taken to avoid conflict, participants taking sides, or outright blocking of compromise.

STEP 4 Lastly, the team creates a final decision statement and verifies that all participants understand and are willing to support their decision.

example of tool application

Increase Customer Contact Time for Complaint Handling   Date: xx/xx/xx

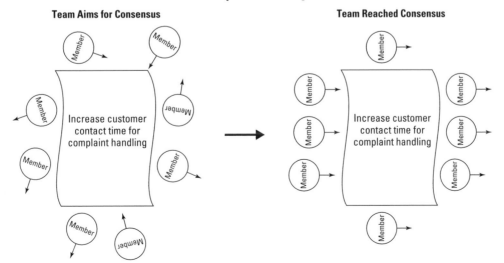

Team Aims for Consensus   Team Reached Consensus

Critical Dialogue

18

AKA **Dialogue**

Idea Generating (IG)

tool description

Team participants use critical dialogue to engage in an open and meaningful flow of thought, exploring and giving serious attention to surfaced ideas. It also provides for common understanding and agreement on solutions to problems or opportunities for improvement. Additionally, critical dialogue gives an opportunity for involving all team participants in the sharing of information and the receiving of valuable feedback.

typical application

- To openly explore the issues and receive constructive feedback during a deep and meaningful sharing of thoughts or ideas on an issue.
- To involve all team participants in a natural flow of conversation leading to a common understanding of the issue or problem at hand.
- To consider ideas or a variety of possible decisions.

problem-solving phase

➡ Select and define problem or opportunity

➡ Identify and analyze causes or potential change

➡ Develop and plan possible solutions or change

Implement and evaluate solution or change

Measure and report solution or change results

Recognize and reward team efforts

links to other tools in *Tool Navigator*™

before
Circles of knowledge
Buzz group
Run-it-by
Different point of view
Fishbowls

after
Consensus decision making
Starbursting
What-if analysis
Barriers-and-aids analysis
Force field analysis (FFA)

notes and key points

- Team facilitators must be careful whenever controversial issues are addressed. Conducting a dialogue about certain issues may result in debating the issues!

step-by-step procedure

STEP 1 The practice of critical dialogue requires an experienced facilitator. The team or group of people seeks out someone who has experience in group dynamics and conflict resolution.

STEP 2 The facilitator arranges a table and chairs to form a circle to establish a sense of equality among participants and to ensure that everyone can see and hear one another.

STEP 3 Next, the facilitator introduces the general concept of critical dialogue, sets a time limit for the session, and asks participants to recall a good, in-depth conversation between equals.

STEP 4 Participants are asked to share their experience and state what characteristics of that conversation made it a good, effective exchange of thoughts.

STEP 5 The facilitator records these characteristics on the flip chart and asks all participants to reflect on the them.

STEP 6 Skillfully, the facilitator introduces a topic to the participants and allows participants to engage in critical dialogue. See example *Team Recognition and Reward*.

STEP 7 From time to time, the facilitator may find it necessary to intervene in order to clarify process steps or assist in reducing confusion or frustration.

STEP 8 Lastly, the facilitator closes the session by asking participants for their ideas or supporting comments and summarizes these on a flip chart for later reference.

example of tool application

Team Recognition and Reward

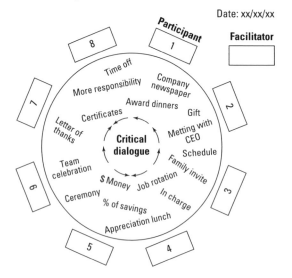

Date: xx/xx/xx

Participant

Facilitator

Nominal Group Technique (NGT)

AKA **Nominal Group Process, Nominal Grouping**

Idea Generating (IG)

tool description

The nominal group technique (NGT) is used primarily to generate ideas, prioritize, and reach team consensus in a very structured, facilitated session. Originally developed by A. Delbecq and A. Van de Ven (1968), NGT has become increasingly popular as a means for participants to have an equal voice in the item or problem selection and decision-making process.

typical application

- To identify and reach consensus on the most important ideas, items, or problems so the team can advance to the next step in a problem-solving effort.
- To prioritize from a list of generated ideas or items with balanced team participation and without conflict.
- To gain participants' commitment by allowing each to fully participate in an idea-generation and -selection process.

problem-solving phase

➥ Select and define problem or opportunity

➥ Identify and analyze causes or potential change

➥ Develop and plan possible solutions or change

Implement and evaluate solution or change

Measure and report solution or change results

Recognize and reward team efforts

links to other tools in *Tool Navigator™*

before

Audience analysis

Circles of knowledge

Brainwriting pool

Phillips 66

Consensus decision making

after

Project planning log

Action and effect diagram (AED)

Force field analysis (FFA)

Action plan

Responsibility matrix

notes and key points

- Although many variations exist, NGT works best if:
  - It is a facilitated session with 8–10 participants.
  - Individual, silent idea generation is used for about 10–15 minutes.
  - Each participant ranks the top five items using a priority/importance/value point scale of 5 for most preferred (highest rank) to 1 for least preferred (lowest rank) items.

step-by-step procedure

STEP 1 The team facilitator displays, on a flip chart, a problem statement or open-ended question. See example *Ideas for Improving Teaming*.

STEP 2 Participants silently generate ideas on provided 3 × 5 cards.

STEP 3 When participants have finished, or after 15 minutes, the facilitator collects and records ideas in a round robin fashion by asking each participant to read his or her written ideas. No evaluation or criticism of ideas is allowed.

STEP 4 Step 3 above is repeated until all ideas have been recorded. Participants may "pass" at any time during this process.

STEP 5 Once the facilitator has recorded all ideas on the flip chart or whiteboard, participants may ask to have some ideas clarified. Ideas may also be modified or combined to promote understanding.

STEP 6 Next, the facilitator asks each participant to list five ideas from the recorded list of ideas that they prefer, writing down only one idea per 3 × 5 card. Individuals rank each idea according to a priority/importance/value point scale, 5 points being the highest and 1 point being the lowest.

STEP 7 The facilitator tabulates the votes and, using the point totals, lists the team's top five ideas and dates the chart as shown in the example.

STEP 8 The team discusses the results and establishes the next steps.

example of tool application

Ideas for Improving Teaming (Team of 10 Participants)

Date xx/xx/xx

Generated List of Ideas	Ranking (1–5)	Top 5
A Job rotation	A–3	3
B Team training	B–5, 4, 3, 5, 5	(22)
C Rewards / recognition	C–5, 2, 4	(11)
D Team facilitation	D–4, 4, 5, 2	(15)
E Open communication	E–3, 3, 3, 1	10
F Involved management	F–3, 1, 2	6
G Job sharing	G–1, 2	3
H Tools training	H–2, 4, 5, 2, 3	(16)
I Cross-functional teams	I–2, 3	5
J Learning communities	J–1, 3	4
K Teaming guidelines	K–1, 4	5
L Time allocation	L–2, 5, 5, 2, 4	(18)
M Self-directed work teams	M–1, 5	6
N Team sharing rally	N–1	1
O IPD teams	O–4, 1	5
P Team newsletters	P–2	2
Q Budget more money for teams	Q–3, 5	8
R Improve evaluation process	R–4, 4, 1, 1	10

Note: Ideas B, L, H, D, and C are the top 5 ideas.

Paired Comparison

AKA **Comparison Grid**

(**Evaluating/Selecting** (ES))

tool description

The paired comparison tool requires all team participants to make choices on several pairs of items (options) such as problems, potential solutions, or activities, in order to arrive at a team decision. In other words, team participants can vote their individual preference, which, when totaled with the other participants' votes, will produce a team ranking of listed items.

typical application

- To quantify team participants' preferred items (choices) for the purpose of arriving at team consensus.
- To force a team to consider the advantages and disadvantages of all listed options, to make comparisons, and to determine the most preferred choice among all options.
- To prioritize a list of problems, potential solutions, or action items.

problem-solving phase

➡ Select and define problem or opportunity

Identify and analyze causes or potential change

➡ Develop and plan possible solutions or change

Implement and evaluate solution or change

Measure and report solution or change results

Recognize and reward team efforts

**links to
other tools in
Tool Navigator™**

before

Weighted voting

Consensus decision making

Phillips 66

Criteria filtering

Countermeasures matrix

after

Project planning log

Action and effect
diagram (AED)

What-if analysis

Cost-benefit analysis

Action plan

notes and key points

- Compare six or fewer items (options) since the number of comparisons increase significantly with the increase of items.
  This can be calculated by: comparisons $= \dfrac{N\,(N-1)}{2}$

# of items	# of comparisons
2	1
3	3
4	6
5	10
6	15
7	21
8	28
9	36
10	45

step-by-step procedure

STEP 1   The team decides to attend a workshop of some quality-related topic. The team's eight participants have choices of Hoshin planning, benchmarking, cycle time management (CTM), and design of experiments (DOE). See example *Workshop Attendance Options*.

STEP 2   A paired comparison grid is drawn on a flip chart. The four training choices are listed in column *Choice* as in the example shown.

STEP 3   Each participant considers every pair of choices and decides which is the preferred choice. One participant tracks the votes as all choices are voted on by all participants. The total votes for each comparison must equal eight, since every participant receives only one vote and *no* participant is allowed to pass!

STEP 4   Upon completion of voting on choices, and once all votes are recorded, the numbers in the pair columns are totaled. The highest number (total) in the totals column reflect the team's preferred choice of training.
Note: The team's decision (total score = 17) calls for cycle time management (CTM) workshop attendance.

STEP 5   Date the final chart.

example of tool application

Workshop Attendance Options

Date: xx/xx/xx

Choice	A or B	A or C	A or D	B or C	B or D	C or D	Totals
A	3	2	5				10
B	5			3	6		14
C		6		5		6	(17)
D			3		2	2	7

Choices
A – Hoshin planning
B – Benchmarking
C – Cycle time management (CTM)
D – Design of experiments (DOE)

Note: Cycle time management is preferred choice.

Point-Scoring Evaluation

AKA **Criteria Rating Form**

Decision Making (DM)

tool description

A point-scoring evaluation rates the importance, value, or preference of listed solutions, factors, or issues by the assignment of points to every alternative, not to exceed a team-set maximum of 100 or 1000 points of all listed alternatives. This rating system effectively supports a team's consensus decision-making effort.

typical application

- To review and rate all listed alternatives.
- To select, by numerical rating, a team's preferred solution, factor, or issue.
- To team-rate the importance, value, or best option of a matrix of factors.

problem-solving phase

Select and define problem or opportunity

➥ Identify and analyze causes or potential change

➥ Develop and plan possible solutions or change

Implement and evaluate solution or change

➥ Measure and report solution or change results

Recognize and reward team efforts

notes and key points

- When point-scoring, use a total of 100 or 1000 points for the distribution across problems, elements, conditions, factors, issues, or ideas.

links to other tools in *Tool Navigator*™

before

Selection matrix

Rating matrix

Ranking matrix

Weighted voting

Solution matrix

after

Problem selection matrix

Project prioritization matrix

Starbursting

Run-it-by

Different point of view

step-by-step procedure

STEP 1 The team facilitator reviews the process of point-scoring with the team.

STEP 2 A point-scoring matrix is drawn on a flip chart or whiteboard. All factors are discussed and recorded in the matrix. See example *Company TQM and Employee Involvement Events*.

STEP 3 Next, the team decides on the maximum number of points to be distributed: 100 or 1000 points. In this example 100 points were distributed.

STEP 4 The facilitator now guides the participants through the evaluation of each listed alternative and arrives at a team rating of points to be assigned to reach the preferred alternative.

STEP 5 The point-scoring matrix is filled and all columns are added to show the highest total. This is the preferred alternative. In this example, 95 points reflect the team's choice.

STEP 6 The matrix is checked for accuracy and dated.

example of tool application

Company TQM and Employee Involvement Events

Date: xx/xx/xx	Type of Event				
Value to the Company	IPD Day lessons learned	Company sharing rally	Company TQM symposium	Learning organization conference	Max. points
Quality improvement	15	20	20	20	25
Shared learning	20	10	15	20	20
Training support	15	10	15	15	15
Teaming communications	15	15	15	15	15
Supports org. objectives	20	10	20	25	25
Totals	85	65	85	95	100

Note: IPD = Integrated product development
TQM = Total quality management

Navigator Tools for Team Creativity and Innovation

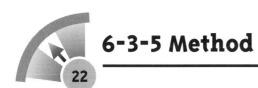

6-3-5 Method

AKA **Round Robin Brainstorming**

Idea Generating (IG)

tool description

The 6-3-5 method is a brainwriting technique that generates and develops ideas by asking six participants to write, within five minutes, three ideas on separate cards. These cards are then passed along to other participants for further refinement or additional ideas.

typical application

- To generate a large list of ideas for problem solving.
- To unlock the creativity in teams.
- To identify process or product-improvement opportunities.
- To refine or build on previously generated ideas.

problem-solving phase

Select and define problem or opportunity

➡ Identify and analyze causes or potential change

➡ Develop and plan possible solutions or change

➡ Implement and evaluate solution or change

Measure and report solution or change results

Recognize and reward team efforts

links to other tools in *Tool Navigator*™

before

Checklist

Checksheet

Observation

Interview technique

Problem specification

after

Criteria filtering

SCAMPER

Cluster analysis

Creativity assessment

Nominal group technique (NGT)

notes and key points

6 — 3 — 5 ←———— (5) Minutes per round

(3) Ideas per participants

(6) Participants per team

step-by-step procedure

STEP 1   A problem statement is shared with a team of six participants. See example *Improve Customer Satisfaction*.

STEP 2   Several blank cards are handed out to each participant with the instruction to generate three ideas (one per card) within five minutes.

STEP 3   Each participant writes three ideas related to the problem statement.

STEP 4   After the five-minute first round, participants pass the cards with written ideas to the person on their left.

STEP 5   The participants read all ideas passed to them, further develop the ideas, or add additional ideas to the previously recorded idea.

STEP 6   After five minutes, the second round is started, using the process as outlined in steps 4–5 above.

STEP 7   This process continues until each participant receives back his or her own card written during round one.

STEP 8   Lastly, all ideas are clustered and recorded. The chart is dated and saved for the next action step.

example of tool application

Improve Customer Satisfaction	Date: xx/xx/xx
External	**Product**
Survey customers	No spare parts
Focus groups	Missing parts
Conduct interviews	Defective products
Random contact	Missing manual
Etc.	Etc.
Internal	**Service**
Complaint file	Make callbacks
Check "returns" records	Be on time
Warranty claims	Forms filled out completely
Ask customer reps	No appointment errors
Sort correspondence	60 day followup
Reorder process	"Know your product"
Ask quality assurance	Accurate information
Shipping problem log	Check Code of Conduct
Etc.	Etc.

Attribute Listing

AKA **N/A**

Idea Generating (IG)

tool description

Developed by Robert Crawford during the 1930s, the attribute listing technique is an idea-generating tool for identifying process, product, and service improvement opportunities. Attributes of a product, service, or process are systematically changed or substituted to search for problem solutions or improvement ideas.

typical application

- To modify product, process, or service characteristics in order to bring problem-solving or improvement ideas to the surface.
- To examine essential problem-related attributes to possibly change or modify them in order to eliminate or reduce the problem.

problem-solving phase

Select and define problem or opportunity

➡ Identify and analyze causes or potential change

➡ Develop and plan possible solutions or change

Implement and evaluate solution or change

Measure and report solution or change results

Recognize and reward team efforts

notes and key points

- To keep a session focused, limit the use of attributes to seven per session.

links to other tools in *Tool Navigator*™

before

Brainstorming

Defect map

Stimulus analysis

Fresh eye

Circles of knowledge

after

Circle of opportunity

Information needs analysis

Opportunity analysis

Creativity assessment

Presentation

step-by-step procedure

STEP 1 First, the problem statement is discussed. See example *Copier Copy Tray Pins Break Frequently*.

STEP 2 All characteristics or attributes of the product, process, or service are listed.

STEP 3 Next, the problem-related, essential characteristics are identified and recorded.

STEP 4 Lastly, the modification or substitution of all characteristics is systematically discussed by team participants. This often results in finding a solution to the problem or an improvement opportunity as shown in the example.

STEP 5 The recorded information is dated.

example of tool application

Problem: Copier Copy Tray Pins Break Frequently   Date: xx/xx/xx

Listing of Characteristics or Attributes:

___ Tray	___ Plastic	___ Strength
✓ Uprights	✓ Metal	___ Diameter
✓ Pins	___ Lock	___ Weight
___ Thickness	___ Hinges	___ Guard
___ Copier holes	___ Size of pin	✓ Pin mounts

First choice: Substitute plastic pin and pin mounts with aluminum parts. Pins will no longer break when tray is bumped.

Second choice: Pins as part of copier frame, holes in uprights of copy tray.

Brainstorming

24

tool description

Brainstorming is an idea-generating tool widely used by teams for identifying problems, alternative solutions to problems, or opportunities for improvement. This tool originated in 1941 by Alex F. Osborne, when his search for creative ideas resulted in an unstructured group process of interactive "brain-storming" that generated more and better ideas than individuals could produce working independently.

typical application

- To unlock the creativity in teams.
- To generate a large list of ideas for problem solving or a list of problem areas for decision making or planning.
- To develop creative alternative solutions.
- To identify improvement opportunities.
- To start innovation in processes, products, and services through team participation.

problem-solving phase

➡ Select and define problem or opportunity
➡ Identify and analyze causes or potential change
   Develop and plan possible solutions or change
   Implement and evaluate solution or change
   Measure and report solution or change results
   Recognize and reward team efforts

links to other tools in *Tool Navigator*™

before

Data collection strategy
Checksheet
Team mirror
Surveying
Interview technique

after

Triple ranking
Multivoting
Nominal group technique (NGT)
SCAMPER
Cluster analysis

notes and key points

- Accept one idea at a time; team members can "pass."
- Encourage members to think of the wildest ideas; they often trigger others!
- Accept expanding, improving, and combining ideas of others (piggy-backing).
- Do not allow instant evaluation of ideas, criticism, or remarks.
- Avoid wandering or side discussions.

step-by-step procedure

STEP 1 Form a team of approximately 6–10 people.

STEP 2 Communicate brainstorming guidelines and set time limit (approximately 15–20 minutes).

STEP 3 State purpose for session; discuss specific problem or topic. See example *Improve Quality.*

STEP 4 Establish a positive, nonthreatening setting and encourage all members to participate in a free-wheeling expression or ideas.

STEP 5 Record, on flip charts, all ideas generated; the emphasis is on quantity, not quality.

STEP 6 When the team has run out of ideas, review and clarify each idea (no discussion).

STEP 7 Allow some time for ideas to incubate.

STEP 8 Identify or prioritize useful ideas.

example of tool application

Improve Quality

Flip chart 1

Session 8/19/xx

Topic: Improve Quality

- More training
- Short due dates
- Inexperience
- No communication
- Missing information
- What is a defect?
- Constant changes
- No inspections
- Too much work
- Many interruptions
- Group conflict
- Incorrect testing

Flip chart 2

Session 8/19/xx

- Lack of proper tools
- Low job satisfaction
- Specifications unclear
- Lack of instructions
- Low morale, motivation
- Lack of metrics
- Involve customers
- Stressful work
- Equipment problems
- Lack of data
- Need problem-solving teams
- No procedures

End of Ideas

Checkerboard Method

AKA **Checkerboard Diagram**

Idea Generating (IG)

tool description

The checkerboard method uses an interrelational matrix to plot interrelationships or the effects of various factors on one another. By combining possible concepts, features, and capabilities, powerful combinations of (or ideas for) feasible new products and services are produced.

typical application

- To generate ideas for new products and services.
- To increase team creativity and innovation.
- To discover process improvement opportunities.
- To identify interrelationships or linkages.

problem-solving phase

➥ Select and define problem or opportunity

➥ Identify and analyze causes or potential change

Develop and plan possible solutions or change

Implement and evaluate solution or change

Measure and report solution or change results

Recognize and reward team efforts

links to other tools in *Tool Navigator*™

before

Brainstorming

Data collection strategy

Observation

Focus group

Checklist

after

Creativity assessment

Run-it-by

Presentation

Consensus decision making

Different point of view

notes and key points

- Do not create matrices greater than vertical (20) × horizontal (25).
- Legend: ◉   High Potential
  - △   Low Potential
  - ☐   (Blank) No Potential

step-by-step procedure

STEP 1   Construct a matrix and determine if available factors are of sufficient detail to insert into the matrix. See example *Telephone Communication Equipment*.

STEP 2   Complete the vertical and horizontal columns as shown in the example.

STEP 3   Match all factors in the vertical columns with the factors in the horizontal column. Not every pairing will be applicable.

STEP 4   As this process of matching continues, rate potential application of feasibility by indicating ◉ for high and △ for low potential.

STEP 5   Finally, date the completed matrix and reach consensus on the next steps.

example of tool application

Telephone Communications Equipment (New Features and Capabilities)

Date: xx/xx/xx

Applications

Equipment	Activity sensor	Smoke alarm	Security loop	Auto dial	Wake up	Door check	All locked	Pet check	Pet exit	Remote check	Room monitor	TV interface	Remote switch	Remote scanner	Gas on/off	Ring neighbor	Time lights	Message transfer	Search file	Inventory DB	Leave message
Phone		△			△			△	○				○	○	○	○	○	○	○	○	○
Video phone	△		○			○	△	○											△	△	△
Speaker phone				○		○		○													△
Fax machine				△									△	○					○	○	△
Answering machine										○				○			○	○			○
Alarm phone	○		○	○	△					△			△	○	△						
Intercom		○				△		△	○		○										○
Recorder	○		△			△				○	○			○				△	○	○	○
Call Distrib														△	○	△	○				△
Timer	△		△	○	○	○	○	△	△	△		△			○		○				○
Transfer		○										△		△	△	△	○			○	△
Scanner										○	○		△	△		△	△		○	○	
Call waiting										○								○			△
Call forward		○											△		○			○			△
Call block										△		△	△			△			△		
Call priority		○	○	△	△					△					○			○		○	

○ = High Potential   △ = Low Potential

Circle of Opportunity

tool description

The circle of opportunity technique is a process of randomly selecting problem-related characteristics or attributes and, by free association, arriving at original and new ideas or possible solutions. As associations are formed or links completed, new relationships, insights, or possibilities produce additional novel ideas for consideration and study by a team.

typical application

- To discover new meanings, relationships, or word associations and, by concentrated study, to produce new thoughts on solving problems or improving products and services.
- To free-associate attributes for the purpose of surfacing original ideas for problem solving or process improvement.
- To selectively study randomly linked word combinations in search of ideas or solutions.

problem-solving phase

Select and define problem or opportunity
➥ Identify and analyze causes or potential change
➥ Develop and plan possible solutions or change
Implement and evaluate solution or change
Measure and report solution or change results
Recognize and reward team efforts

links to other tools in *Tool Navigator*™

before
Attribute listing
Fresh eye
Mental imaging
Forced choice
Circumrelation

after
Stimulus analysis
Idea advocate
Opportunity analysis
Information needs analysis
Value analysis

notes and key points

- To ensure randomness, a pair of dice is needed to select characteristics or attributes listed around a closed circle (circle of opportunity).

step-by-step procedure

STEP 1   The team facilitator displays a problem statement to the team participants. See example *Problem: Frequent Machine Downtime.*

STEP 2   A circle of opportunity is constructed as shown in the example.

STEP 3   Problem-related characteristics are identified by the team. The facilitator records these around the twelve circle of opportunity segments.

STEP 4   The facilitator throws one die to determine the first characteristic, then throws both dice to determine the second characteristic.

STEP 5   The team collectively free-associates using individual and combined word characteristics. The facilitator records on flip charts any associations and resulting ideas or insights as they are produced by the participants.

STEP 6   Connections or links to the problem are surfaced and analyzed. Any thoughts that may help to finalize a solution to the problem are also recorded.

STEP 7   Collectively, the participants produce a potential solution statement as seen in the example.

STEP 8   The circle of opportunity is dated and shown to the process owner.

example of tool application

Problem: Frequent Machine Downtime   Date: xx/xx/xx

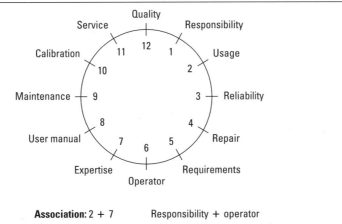

Association: 2 + 7   Responsibility + operator
Best idea: Include machine servicing
Association: 10 + 8   Maintenance + expertise
Best idea: Train operators in maintenance

Potential Solution: Rewrite the machine operator job description to include the servicing and maintenance of the equipment. This will prevent excessive work delays due to machine downtime.

Circumrelation

27

AKA **Forced Relationship Method**

Idea Generating (IG)

tool description

The circumrelation method is an idea generation tool developed by Frank Laverty. Using three freely spinning disks, each with factors recorded in respective sections, forced relationships are possible by rotating the disks so that different factors, one from each disk, are lined up to form a combination of factors. Combinations are evaluated for useful ideas or potential solutions.

typical application

- To examine related problem factors by combining three different factors at a time in an attempt to produce some ideas for problem resolution.
- To discover novel ideas for process improvement.
- To utilize a systemic approach to problem solving.

problem-solving phase

➥ Select and define problem or opportunity
➥ Identify and analyze causes or potential change
  Develop and plan possible solutions or change
  Implement and evaluate solution or change
  Measure and report solution or change results
  Recognize and reward team efforts

links to other tools in *Tool Navigator™*

before
Problem specification
Brainstorming
Phillips 66
Brainwriting pool
Focus group

after
Criteria filtering
Run-it-by
Different point of view
Consensus decision making
Wildest idea technique

notes and key points

Circumrelator Assembly

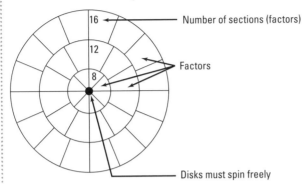

- For individual or team idea generation.
- A basic circumrelator has three disks measuring 3, 5, and 7 inches in diameter. A fourth disk is optional.
- Disks are divided into 8, 12, and 16 sections. Multiplying $8 \times 12 \times 16 = 1536$ factor combinations or forced relationships.

step-by-step procedure

STEP 1   The team (or individual) reviews the previously specified problem.

STEP 2   Three major areas related to the problem are identified. See example *Circumrelation: Reduce Defect Level*. People issues, equipment maintenance, and defect types are all related to a reduce defect level.

STEP 3   The team brainstorms factors for each major area. This process is continued until the team stops generating factors.

STEP 4   Using the nominal group technique (NGT), the team reduces the number of generated factors in each major area to 8-12-16.

STEP 5   Factors are now recorded in the sections of the three major areas on the three disks.

STEP 6   The search for idea-producing combinations calls for the rotation of one disk at a time, lining up different combinations (forced relationships).

STEP 7   The team assesses all combinations and records any ideas that warrant further consideration in order to solve the problem. See idea in example shown.

example of tool application

Reduce Defect Level

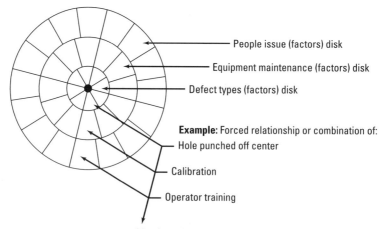

People issue (factors) disk

Equipment maintenance (factors) disk

Defect types (factors) disk

Example: Forced relationship or combination of:

Hole punched off center

Calibration

Operator training

Idea for reducing defect level: Train operators to be able to calibrate equipment

Double Reversal

tool description

The double reversal is a reversed thinking process that allows teams to continue with idea generating after they have run out of ideas or simply have found no novel way of looking at the problem. This tool requires an issue, idea, or goal to be reversed or stated in a negative form in order to gain more ideas of what could cause the problem. Reversing again each reversed idea should produce potential action steps to consider in the problem solution phase.

typical application

- To identify the less obvious ideas for problem resolution.
- To expand the list of ideas developed during a classical brainstorming session.
- To search for additional process or quality improvement opportunities.
- To recover from an unproductive brainstorming effort.
- To further clarify a problem to gain more solution ideas.

problem-solving phase

➡ Select and define problem or opportunity

➡ Identify and analyze causes or potential change

➡ Develop and plan possible solutions or change

   Implement and evaluate solution or change

   Measure and report solution or change results

   Recognize and reward team efforts

links to other tools in *Tool Navigator*™

before

Brainstorming

Round robin brainstorming

Focus group

Crawford slip method

Brainwriting

after

Sticking dots

Opportunity analysis

Consensus decision making

Multivoting

Process selection matrix

notes and key points

- Reversed also means, for this tool application, the negated or negative form of the idea presented.

step-by-step procedure

STEP 1 The team reviews the session objective or desired improvement goal. See example *Reduce the Percentage of "No Shows" in Scheduled Training Workshops*.

STEP 2 A list of ideas, previously brainstormed, is displayed and discussed.

STEP 3 The next action taken is to reverse the objective. See example *Increase the percentage of "No Shows" in Scheduled Training Workshops*.

STEP 4 The team now brainstorms how to make the condition or problem worse—the reversed or negative form of the objective.

STEP 5 Once the reversed ideas have been recorded, the team reverses again all ideas—the double reversal process.

STEP 6 The final step is to add all newly developed ideas to the previous list. The team now has some fresh, different potential solutions to the problem.

example of tool application

Reduce the Percentage of "No-Shows" in Scheduled Training Workshops

Date: xx/xx/xx

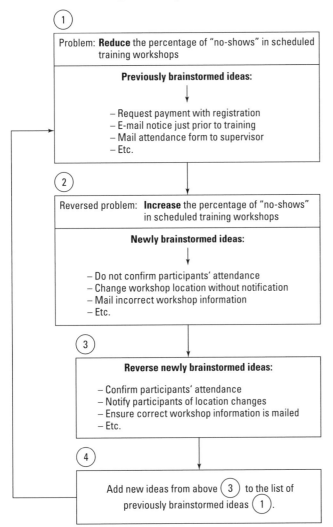

(1)

Problem: **Reduce** the percentage of "no-shows" in scheduled training workshops

Previously brainstormed ideas:

- Request payment with registration
- E-mail notice just prior to training
- Mail attendance form to supervisor
- Etc.

(2)

Reversed problem: **Increase** the percentage of "no-shows" in scheduled training workshops

Newly brainstormed ideas:

- Do not confirm participants' attendance
- Change workshop location without notification
- Mail incorrect workshop information
- Etc.

(3)

Reverse newly brainstormed ideas:

- Confirm participants' attendance
- Notify participants of location changes
- Ensure correct workshop information is mailed
- Etc.

(4)

Add new ideas from above (3) to the list of previously brainstormed ideas (1).

Note: The result is a **longer** list of brainstormed ideas.

Forced Association

29

AKA **Direct Association**

Idea Generating (IG)

tool description

The forced association technique is an idea generation tool that allows a team to associate or connect pairs of unrelated concepts, ideas, or terms to search for potential solutions, improved processes, or new products and services.

typical application

- To generate ideas for new products and services.
- To provide an opportunity for team creativity and innovation.
- To allow an individual or team to think in many different ways.

problem-solving phase

Select and define problem or opportunity

➡ Identify and analyze causes or potential change

➡ Develop and plan possible solutions or change

Implement and evaluate solution or change

Measure and report solution or change results

➡ Recognize and reward team efforts

notes and key points

- Brainstorm several lists of 10 concepts, ideas, and terms. This enables a team to significantly increase the number of possible connections.

links to other tools in *Tool Navigator™*

before

Brainstorming

Brainwriting pool

Phillips 66

Reverse brainstorming

Focus group

after

Criteria filtering

Run-it-by

Different point of view

Consensus decision making

Team process assessment

step-by-step procedure

STEP 1 The team brainstorms four or five lists of 10 unrelated concepts, ideas, or terms.

STEP 2 The team then mixes all items of randomly selected items and assigns them to two columns. See example *Sports with Marketing Research*.

STEP 3 The team systematically scans each pair and checks for emerging ideas.

STEP 4 This process continues and potential ideas are recorded.

STEP 5 Lastly, the team performs criteria filtering to produce a list of high potential or great ideas.

example of tool application

Sports with Marketing Research   Date: xx/xx/xx

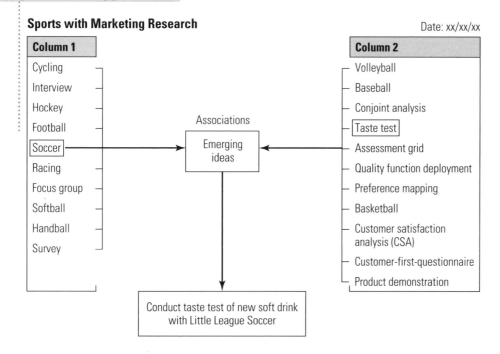

Fresh Eye

AKA **N/A**

Idea Generating (IG)

tool description

The fresh eye technique searches for new or unique ideas to a previously analyzed problem. Process owners often have difficulties looking at a problem from an unbiased view. The fresh eye technique allows other, uninvolved people to generate and pass on some innovative ideas on how to solve the problem.

typical application

- To stimulate a fresh look at the problem.
- To search for unique or more promising ideas to solve a problem or improve a process.
- To involve outside-the-process people in the idea generation.

problem-solving phase

➡ Select and define problem or opportunity
➡ Identify and analyze causes or potential change
➡ Develop and plan possible solutions or change
   Implement and evaluate solution or change
   Measure and report solution or change results
   Recognize and reward team efforts

notes and key points

- There are two variations of the fresh eye technique:
  - Individual or team search for other problem-solving ideas.
  - Asking people outside the team or process to think of problem-solving ideas.

links to other tools in *Tool Navigator™*

before
Reverse brainstorming
Double reversal
Pin cards technique
Activity analysis
Brainstorming

after
Consensus decision making
Different point of view
Action plan
Run-it-by
Presentation

step-by-step procedure

STEP 1   The team decides to use the fresh eye technique to improve the chances of discovering additional, unique, or innovative ideas.

STEP 2   The previously developed problem statement is rechecked for content and clarity. The team may decide to restate the problem in different, yet clear and concise terms. See example *Improve the Effectiveness of Team Training.*

STEP 3   The problem statement is typed and distributed to some people who are interested in assisting but who are outside the problem or have little experience with the undesirable situation.

STEP 4   After approximately one week, all ideas from outsiders are collected and their potential evaluated by the team.

STEP 5   Finally, the team may find that this process may give them some other fresh ideas or build on their previous list of ideas.

example of tool application

Improve the Effectivness of Team Training

List of previously generated ideas

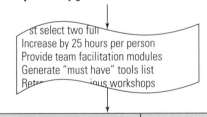

st select two full
Increase by 25 hours per person
Provide team facilitation modules
Generate "must have" tools list
Retr_____ious workshops

"Fresh Eye" Ideas	Date: xx/xx/xx
Perform "just-in-time" training	
Allow team participants to input into the training process	
Convert structured modules into team exercises	
Use case studies of successful teams as background for training module development	
Place training into an employee's personal development plan	

Idea Borrowing

31

AKA **N/A**

Idea Generating (IG)

tool description

The idea borrowing technique allows team participants to bring to the surface ideas from inside and outside the organization or through their own creativity. Team-established criteria is used to rate and select the top-rated ideas to consider implementing.

typical application

- To surface best practices, technological innovations, and perceived good ideas.
- To supplement brainstorming and benchmarking activities.
- To stimulate the creativity of employees.

problem-solving phase

➡ Select and define problem or opportunity

Identify and analyze causes or potential change

➡ Develop and plan possible solutions or change

Implement and evaluate solution or change

Measure and report solution or change results

➡ Recognize and reward team efforts

links to other tools in *Tool Navigator*™

before

Information needs analysis

Benchmarking

Fresh eye

Wildest idea technique

Mental imaging

after

Idea advocate

Run-it-by

Creativity assessment

Why/how charting

Presentation

136

40 Tools for Cross-Functional Teams

notes and key points

- Suggested idea selection criteria and scales:

Source of Idea	Potential Use	Estimated Implementation Costs
3 = Self (original)	5 = High	3 = Acceptable
2 = Internal	3 = Medium	2 = Marginal
1 = External	1 = Low	1 = Unacceptable

- To select the best idea, multiply columns Source × Potential × Costs. Rank ideas: highest total = best idea.

step-by-step procedure

STEP 1   The team facilitator reviews the idea borrowing technique with the team and answers any questions participants may have at this point.

STEP 2   Participants silently list their ideas on provided paper. Ideas may be best practices, innovations, untried employee suggestions, benchmarking discoveries, and so forth.

STEP 3   After some predetermined idea-generation time, the facilitator asks participants to share their ideas. All ideas are listed on a whiteboard or flip charts.

STEP 4   The team discusses all ideas and, through consensus, identifies the top 15–20 ideas. The facilitator prepares a matrix containing this final list of ideas. See example *List of Ideas to Upgrade Employee Training*.

STEP 5   Next, the team decides on a set of criteria and associated scales to be used to rate all ideas.

STEP 6   All ideas are rated and ranked in accordance with the established criteria, as shown in this example.

STEP 7   Finally, the team prepares a presentation for presenting the ideas to upper management.

example of tool application

List of Ideas to Upgrade Employee Training

Description of Ideas	Source of Idea	Potential Use of Idea	Estimated Implementation Costs	Idea Selection	
				Total	Rank
Exchange and/or share trainers with other organizations	3	1	2	6	3
Ask employees to review the literature and present on contemporary topics	2	3	3	(18)	1
Make available internet access for technology update	1	5	1	5	4
Contract university faculty for special topic sessions	1	3	1	3	6
Engage recognized company subject matter experts to present on specific skill areas	1	5	3	15	2
Ask employees to team-develop their own training modules	2	1	2	4	5

Note: (1) **Source**   **Potential**   **Cost**
        3 = self   5 = high   3 = acceptable
        2 = internal   3 = medium   2 = marginal
        1 = external   1 = low   1 = unacceptable

      (2) Multiply columns: Source × Potential × Costs

      (3) (18) highest total is best idea.

Mental Imaging

32

Idea Generating (IG)

tool description

The mental imaging technique suggests using imagination or visualization to identify key relationships in problem areas, solutions to problems, or ways to process improvement. Any creative ideas are switched or associated with a different condition process, product, or service to search for a breakthrough idea.

typical application

- To create experiences or images of potential solutions to problems.
- To visualize the ideal outcome or situation.
- To identify barriers to solutions or improved performance.

problem-solving phase

Select and define problem or opportunity
➡ Identify and analyze causes or potential change
➡ Develop and plan possible solutions or change
Implement and evaluate solution or change
Measure and report solution or change results
Recognize and reward team efforts

notes and key points

- Select a quiet and comfortable workplace or location.
- Ensure that there is little chance of interruptions during the mental imaging session.

links to other tools in *Tool Navigator*™

before

Fresh eye

Wishful thinking

Morphological analysis

Stimulus analysis

Mind flow

after

Creativity assessment

Wildest idea technique

What-if analysis

Checkerboard diagram

Different point of view

step-by-step procedure

STEP 1   The first task for this process is to locate a quiet place that will not be subjected to frequent interruptions.

STEP 2   Mental imaging works best if a person or a team first performs some relaxation techniques.

STEP 3   Next, imagination or visualization of the solved problem, ideal conditions, or drastic improvements take place. Ideas are generated and are recorded on slips of paper. See example *Tool Navigator Marketing*.

STEP 4   After approximately 30–45 minutes, all generated images are discussed. From this exercise, some general idea or trend will emerge as the ideal or most effective solution or improvement.

STEP 5   The team continues to identify the gaps between the existing to ideal situation and starts a discussion on how to reach the ideal situation.

STEP 6   A preliminary action plan is developed that describes the best idea(s) and how they could be implemented, as shown in the example.

example of tool application

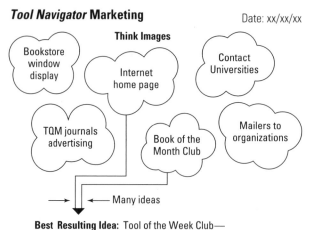

Tool Navigator **Marketing**   Date: xx/xx/xx

Think Images

Bookstore window display

Internet home page

Contact Universities

TQM journals advertising

Book of the Month Club

Mailers to organizations

→   ← Many ideas

Best Resulting Idea: Tool of the Week Club— Administered via internet, would take approximately 4.5 years to acquire all 222 tools.

Morphological Analysis

33

Idea Generating (IG)

tool description

Morphological analysis is a tool used to surface new or improved products or services. Usually three or more dimensions are identified for a particular subject or problem, and variations for each dimension are brainstormed to develop lists of attributes. By scanning the attributes in each dimension, useful or interesting combinations are discovered that may form a new or improved product or service, or may be the solution to a problem.

typical application

- To discover new or improved products or services.
- To combine various attributes in search for a solution to a problem.
- To surface useful ideas by combining different variations of identified dimensions of a product or service.

problem-solving phase

➡ Select and define problem or opportunity

➡ Identify and analyze causes or potential change

➡ Develop and plan possible solutions or change

Implement and evaluate solution or change

Measure and report solution or change results

Recognize and reward team efforts

links to other tools in *Tool Navigator™*

before

Attribute listing

Forced choice

Circumrelation

Circle of opportunity

Forced association

after

Creativity assessment

Mental imaging

Checkerboard method

Idea advocate

Presentation

notes and key points

- Three- or four-dimensional morphological analyses are the most common approaches. A dimension is further defined as a characteristic, variation, factor, or aspect.

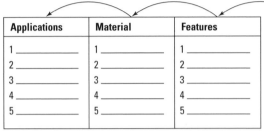

Applications	Material	Features
1 _____	1 _____	1 _____
2 _____	2 _____	2 _____
3 _____	3 _____	3 _____
4 _____	4 _____	4 _____
5 _____	5 _____	5 _____

These *dimensions* are also referred to as *parameters* or *attribute listings*

Note: This example has three dimensions with five variations in each: 5 × 5 × 5 = 125 possible combinations.

step-by-step procedure

STEP 1   The team selects a problem, product, or service to be analyzed. See example *Additional Uses for Picture Frames*.

STEP 2   Dimensions are identified and recorded as headings on flip charts.

STEP 3   Next, the team brainstorms attributes (variations) of each dimension. The facilitator clarifies each response, if needed, and records responses on the flip chart. This process continues until the team stops generating attributes.

STEP 4   The other dimensions are brainstormed and attributes listed on respective flip charts.

STEP 5   The facilitator moves all flip charts close together and participants combine the possibilities by linking the various useful attributes listed on each flip chart (one per flip chart or column).

STEP 6   Useful, potential, or interesting combinations are marked using different colors of flip chart markers.

STEP 7   Date all flip charts.

example of tool application

Additional Uses for
Picture Frames

Date: xx/xx/xx

Applications	Material	Features
Calendar	Wood	Attachable
Picture	Plastic	Adjustable
Bulletin	Brass	Expandable
Sign	Styrofoam	Reshapeable
Poster	Cardboard	Interlocking
Flag	Sheet metal	Hang
		Stand
Shelf	Glass	
Clock	Plywood	Mountable

Note: Many interesting combinations are possible.

SCAMPER

34

tool description

The SCAMPER tool is an outcome of the creative facilitation work performed by Alex F. Osborne in the 1950s. Consisting of a checklist of simple questions, this tool can be used by a team to explore the issues and question everything to formulate new, fresh ideas. Problem-solving teams often produce many solution ideas when responding to the SCAMPER questions asked.

typical application

- To question and identify improvement opportunities for processes, products, and services.
- To formulate alternative ideas for problem solving or process change.
- To produce a large number of solution ideas.

problem-solving phase

➡ Select and define problem or opportunity

➡ Identify and analyze causes or potential change

➡ Develop and plan possible solutions or change

Implement and evaluate solution or change

Measure and report solution or change results

Recognize and reward team efforts

links to other tools in *Tool Navigator*™

before
Brainstorming
Checksheet
Defect map
Pareto chart
Events log

after
Starbursting
Countermeasures matrix
Problem analysis
Process analysis
Solution matrix

notes and key points

- The mnemonic SCAMPER (developed by Bob Eberle) stands for:

S - Substitute?

C - Combine?

A - Adapt?

M - Modify? Magnify?

P - Put to other uses?

E - Eliminate? Minimize?

R - Reverse? Rearrange?

step-by-step procedure

STEP 1   Assemble a representative team with knowledge of the topic, issue, or problem to be analyzed. See example *Defective Flashlight Switch*.

STEP 2   One by one, the idea-spurring SCAMPER questions are presented to the team.

STEP 3   Participants discuss the questions and formulate ideas. Responses are recorded as the SCAMPER checklist or questions are completed.

example of tool application

Defective Flashlight Switch

SCAMPER Questions—Defective Switch   Date xx/xx/xx
S – Can we *substitute* a more reliable switch?
C – *Combine* slide switch assembly with the signaling button?
A – What ideas or concepts can be *adapted* from other similar switches?
M – *Modify* the switch to have fewer parts?
P – Can the switch be *put* to other uses?
E – Can the switch be *eliminated* or exchanged?
R – How can we *rearrange* the components of the switch to a more robust design?

Semantic Intuition

35

Idea Generating (IG)

tool description

Semantic intuition is an idea-generating tool used by teams to create a product or process invention by combining words from two or three previously brainstormed lists all related to a problem area. Developed by the Battelle Institute (Frankfurt), the idea is to back into an invention by first naming it, then checking to see if it is feasible to implement. This is the reverse of the usual process of inventing first and then implementing.

typical application

- To discover an invention by word association.
- To search for creative solutions to a problem.
- To identify word combinations that may result in a new product, process, or service.

problem-solving phase

➡ Select and define problem or opportunity

➡ Identify and analyze causes or potential change

Develop and plan possible solutions or change

Implement and evaluate solution or change

Measure and report solution or change results

Recognize and reward team efforts

notes and key points

- Two- and three-word combinations may increase the probability of finding inventions.
- For use by individuals or teams of 6–8 participants.

links to other tools in *Tool Navigator™*

before

Brainstorming

Forced association

Forced choice

Idea borrowing

Round robin brainstorming

after

Analogy and metaphor

Checkerboard method

Creativity assessment

Run-it-by

Presentation

step-by-step procedure

STEP 1 The first step requires the team to define a problem area. See example *Lack of Funds to Purchase Training Equipment for Each Classroom*; Solution: Portable Flip Chart Easel.

STEP 2 The team brainstorms two or three wordlists that are linked or related to the problem. Wordlists are displayed side-by-side for the team to view during this process.

STEP 3 Next, words are combined or associated to form new names or potential ideas. The team systematically scans all wordlists in order to surface many combinations.

STEP 4 Discussions take place on word combinations that need further exploration. An attempt is made to visualize a new product, process, or service.

STEP 5 Potential inventions are listed by circling the words and connecting the words with lines (links) drawn from one wordlist to the other(s), as shown in the example.

example of tool application

Lack of Funds to Purchase Training Equipment for Each Classroom
Solution: Portable Flip Chart Easel

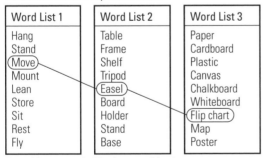

From: Move–easel–flip chart combination
To: Portable—easel—flip chart invention

Stimulus Analysis

36

AKA **N/A**

Idea Generating (IG)

tool description

Developed by the Battelle Institute in Frankfurt, Germany, the stimulus analysis tool provides a method of generating problem-solving ideas using unrelated words or objects as potential idea sources. Characteristics of previously brainstormed words or objects are identified and described and then used to stimulate the surfacing of ideas that hold a potential solution to the problem.

typical application

- To stimulate the generation of ideas for problem-solving efforts.
- To provide a creativity and innovation method for teams.
- To identify product, process, or service-improvement opportunities.

problem-solving phase

→ Select and define problem or opportunity

→ Identify and analyze causes or potential change

→ Develop and plan possible solutions or change

Implement and evaluate solution or change

Measure and report solution or change results

Recognize and reward team efforts

links to other tools in Tool Navigator™

before
Brainstorming
Circle of opportunity
Circumrelation
Wildest idea technique
Wishful thinking

after
Creativity assessment
Idea advocate
Circles of knowledge
Information needs analysis
Presentation

notes and key points

- Concentrate on one unrelated word or object at a time. If no useful ideas are generated, move on to the next word and repeat the process.

step-by-step procedure

STEP 1   A problem, issue, or concern is displayed to the team. Some discussion or clarification of the technique takes place.

STEP 2   The facilitator prepares three flip charts with headings of *Idea Source*, *Characteristics*, and *Ideas*.

STEP 3   The team brainstorms 8–10 stimulus words or objects that are unrelated to the problem. The facilitator records these on the prepared flip chart. See example *Shared Copier—In Use When Needed*.

STEP 4   Next, the team identifies characteristics such as material, parts, uses, features, etc., for the first word, as shown in the example.

STEP 5   Characteristics are recorded and discussed, compared, analyzed, and connected in thought; these are also connected in the search for a problem solution or an improvement idea for the stated problem, issue, or concern.

STEP 6   This process continues until the team has exhausted all possibilities with the particular word or object.

STEP 7   The facilitator records useful ideas and restarts the process with the next word or object.

STEP 8   Finally, all meaningful, high potential solutions are recorded for further analysis and action.

example of tool application

Shared Copier—In Use When Needed

Date xx/xx/xx

Idea Source	Characteristics	Ideas
File Cabinet	– Contains files – Four drawers – Is metallic – Has handles – Name plates – Can be locked – Stores info – Stands upright	– Can a copier be called and store repro requests – Call copier to check if not in use; receive "Not In Use" tone
Fax Machine	– Make calls – Receive calls – Has memory – Gives date/time – Makes copies – Stores calls – Stores documents – Remote access – Signals	– Have fax send document to copier for reproduction. Copier stores information and rings back when repro job is completed.
Desk	– Wooden	

Wildest Idea Technique

37

AKA **Wildest Idea Thinking**

Idea Generating (IG)

tool description

Of all the different variations of brainstorming, the wildest idea technique is perhaps the most challenging and creative activity. This tool encourages participants to perform out-of-the box brainstorming with the goal of generating truly outrageous and wild ideas. The underlying application of this tool is to discover breakthrough ideas for process, product, or service improvements.

typical application

- To generate unusual and wild ideas that normal brainstorming methods do not.
- To collect "anything goes" ideas for the purpose of finding practical applications or solutions that normally do not surface during regular sessions.
- To promote creative thinking among brainstorming participants.

problem-solving phase

➡ Select and define problem or opportunity

Identify and analyze causes or potential change

➡ Develop and plan possible solutions or change

Implement and evaluate solution or change

Measure and report solution or change results

Recognize and reward team efforts

notes and key points

- An experienced facilitator can promote more direct participation in this process by applying lessons learned from previous facilitation of round robin, classical, or reversed brainstorming sessions.
- Some wild ideas may need on-the-spot clarification in order to make sense later.

---

links to other tools in *Tool Navigator™*

before

Brainstorming

Mental imaging

Round robin brainstorming

Interview technique

Buzz group

after

Starbursting

Thematic content analysis

Consensus decision making

Criteria filtering

Multivoting

---

step-by-step procedure

STEP 1   The facilitator introduces this brainstorming variation and provides a rationale for using it.

STEP 2   Brainstorming is started by the facilitator's displaying of several outrageous or impossible ideas to a stated topic, issue, or problem. See example *Employee/Team Recognition and Reward.*

STEP 3   Participants generate other wild, crazy ideas or hitchhike on others already mentioned.

STEP 4   The facilitator records ideas on the flip chart and monitors the process closely to ensure that participants do not revert back to generating more conventional ideas.

STEP 5   The process is continued until all participants run out of wild ideas. The final list of ideas is dated and saved for next steps.

example of tool application

Employee/Team Recognition and Reward   Date xx/xx/xx
– Team gets 10% of profits
– "Honorary Executive" title
– Team success on E-mail distribution
– Teams determine recognition/reward
– Give "markers"
– Open doors for 2 days
– Team goes on cruise
– Job rotation for a week
– President of the company for a day

Navigator Tools to Assess Team Creativity

Creativity Assessment

38

AKA **Creative Evaluation**

Evaluating/Selecting (ES)

tool description

Developed by Leo Moore, the creativity assessment technique is applied as a sorting and rating process to a long list of brainstormed ideas. It should help teams with evaluation and categorization by selecting ideas on the basis of predetermined criteria.

typical application

- To categorize a list of generated ideas using team-established criteria.
- To evaluate and sort ideas into groups.
- To screen ideas or solutions considered for implementation.

problem-solving phase

➡ Select and define problem or opportunity

➡ Identify and analyze causes or potential change

➡ Develop and plan possible solutions or change

Implement and evaluate solution or change

Measure and report solution or change results

Recognize and reward team efforts

links to other tools in *Tool Navigator*™

before

Brainstorming

Round robin brainstorming

Brainwriting pool

Pin cards technique

Criteria filtering

after

Consensus decision making

Cluster analysis

Solution matrix

Selection matrix

Presentation

notes and key points

- The categorization scheme is often dependent on the type of data and the situation encountered.
  - Ideas can be categorized into levels of difficulty using Roman numerals for designating levels, such as:

    I = easy to do; II = hard to do; III = most difficult to do
  - Other criteria can be used to determine value, importance, cost, and resources required:

    I = few resources required; II = considerable resources required;

    III = a great many resources required.

step-by-step procedure

STEP 1   The team's facilitator displays flip charts of previously brainstormed ideas. See example *Improve Quality*.

STEP 2   The participants establish the criteria for assessment. In this example, the criteria are easy to do, hard to do, and most difficult to do.

STEP 3   The facilitator writes the respective category headings on three flip charts, and participants evaluate and organize ideas into the three categories as shown in this example.

STEP 4   After all ideas have been categorized, the three resulting categories I–III are reviewed and dated.

STEP 5   Lastly, the team presents the three idea categories to upper management for further evaluation and action.

example of tool application

Improve Quality

Flip chart 1

Session 8/19/xx

Topic: Improve Quality

- More training
- Short due dates
- Inexperience
- No communication
- Missing info
- What is a defect?
- Constant changes
- No inspections
- Too much work
- Many interruptions
- Group conflict
- Incorrect testing

Flip chart 2

Session 8/19/xx

- Lack of proper tools
- Low job satisfaction
- Specifications unclear
- Lack of instructions
- Low morale, motivation
- Lack of metrics
- Involve customers
- Stressful work
- Equipment problems
- Lack of data
- Need problem-solving teams
- No procedures

End of Ideas

I – Easy to Do

- Missing info
- No inspections
- Too much work
- Many interruptions
- Incorrect testing
- Lack of proper tools
- Specifications unclear
- Equipment problems

II – Hard to Do

- More training
- Inexperience
- No communications
- What is a defect?
- Constant changes
- Lack of instructions
- Lack of metrics
- Stressful work
- Lack of data
- Need PS teams
- No procedures

III – Most Difficult to Do

- Short due dates
- Group conflict
- Low job satisfaction
- Low morale, motivation
- Involve customers

Stage Eight

Navigator Tools for Team Recognition and Reward

Different Point of View

Planning/Presenting (PP)

tool description

The different point of view tool is ideal for a team to used to acquire a second opinion or an outsider's view to verify that a potential solution to a problem has been well thought out. Another application of this tool is to predict how other people may react to a team's proposal or what may be asked during a team's presentation.

typical application

- To allow further clarification of the problem.
- To solicit more information to gain further insight into issues, concerns, or consequences.
- To determine if important issues have been overlooked.
- To consider the view or input of people outside the team.

problem-solving phase

Select and define problem or opportunity

Identify and analyze causes or potential change

➡ Develop and plan possible solutions or change

Implement and evaluate solution or change

Measure and report solution or change results

➡ Recognize and reward team efforts

links to other tools in *Tool Navigator*™

before

Double reversal

Reverse brainstorming

Delphi method

Focus group

Presentation

after

Thematic content analysis

Gap analysis

Team rating

Solution matrix

Response matrix analysis

notes and key points

- Suggested groups to provide different points of view are users, customers, process owners, subject matter experts, people affected by a change, and people who are responsible for the work unit or implementation activities.

step-by-step procedure

STEP 1   The team has developed a proposed solution to a problem, an action plan, or a process improvement opportunity. See example *Changing the Parts Data Base Update Procedure.*

STEP 2   The team determines the people whose points of view may differ on the basis of position, work duties, interests, etc. A copy of the proposal is distributed to selected people or groups as shown in the example.

STEP 3   Different points of view are collected from the selected people and groups.

STEP 4   The next activity requires the team to complete a thematic content analysis to identify common strands of thought, clusters of similar ideas, recommendations for revisions, or agreement on possible action items.

STEP 5   Having identified essential revisions based on the different points of view, the team completes the revised work and presents a finalized proposal or action plan for implementation.

example of tool application

Changing the Parts Database
Update Procedure

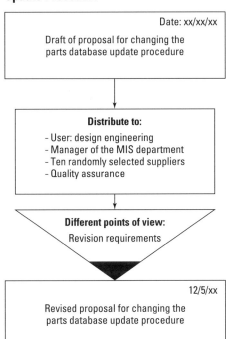

Date: xx/xx/xx

Draft of proposal for changing the
parts database update procedure

Distribute to:

- User: design engineering
- Manager of the MIS department
- Ten randomly selected suppliers
- Quality assurance

Different points of view:

Revision requirements

12/5/xx

Revised proposal for changing the
parts database update procedure

Presentation

40

tool description

A presentation is an activity from which both team participants and process owners receive benefits. Presentations show a team's progress, achievement, or a proposal for action. Another purpose for a presentation is to obtain approvals and commitments from the organization's decision makers.

typical application

- To report on a team's progress.
- To communicate essential information.
- To update management on projects, changes, or potential problem areas.

problem-solving phase

Select and define problem or opportunity
Identify and analyze causes or potential change
Develop and plan possible solutions or change
Implement and evaluate solution or change
➥ Measure and report solution or change results
➥ Recognize and reward team efforts

links to other tools in *Tool Navigator™*

before
Audience analysis
Information needs analysis
Case study
Critical incident
Brainstorming

after
Different point of view
Run-it-by
Starbursting
Interview technique
Resource requirement matrix

notes and key points

- When preparing and making a presentation avoid the following:
  - Unnecessary information
  - Unfamiliar jargon or acronyms
  - Putting others on the spot
  - Blaming people or departments
  - Bypassing levels of responsibility
  - Visuals with information overload

step-by-step procedure

STEP 1 Periodically a team decides to present the status of its problem-solving efforts. A presentation can also be arranged by any group that wishes to communicate important information to a particular audience.

STEP 2 The team selects a participant to take overall responsibility to coordinate the activities required to develop and conduct the presentation.

STEP 3 The presentation is developed using a checklist. See example *Preparing a Presentation*.

STEP 4 The rest of the team assists in the completing of the action items as shown in the checklist.

STEP 5 The presenter rehearses the presentation with the team. This provides the opportunity for team members to critique the presentation and then rehearse and fine tune it for maximum effectiveness.

example of tool application

Preparing a Presentation

Checklist for Effective Presentations
☐ Identify the objective of the presentation
☐ Analyze the audience
☐ Estimate time requirements
☐ Construct the presentation
– Introduction — state importance
– Body — focus on main points
– Conclusion — summarize essentials
☐ Assemble supporting information
☐ Create visuals
☐ Develop handouts
☐ Invite process owners, key decision makers
☐ Check out facilities (adequate chairs and tables)
☐ Check out A/V equipment (good working order)
☐ Anticipate and prepare for questions
☐ Start and stop on time!

A Nontechnical Introduction

Six sigma quality can be defined at two different, yet closely related, levels. At the managerial level, we can regard six sigma as a customer-driven improvement process that is the framework for managing quality throughout the organization. This means that resources and company commitment must support an ongoing effort to reduce variation in every aspect of the business—contract proposals, product design, materials and components from suppliers, internal processes, products and services, and administrative support.

At the operational level, six sigma can be linked directly to the measurement and statistical reporting of quantitative and qualitative metrics. Six sigma is a virtual "zero defects" approach to quality. For every million opportunities to create a defect, only 3.4 defects may occur! This equates to a yield of 99.99966 percent! The measurement uses the standard normal distribution curve (NDC) and overlays (shifts) a process mean (average) of 1.5 sigma to account for process drift in either direction of the curve and its specification limits. Out-of-specification results, with a process mean shift, would indicate:

66,810	defects for	3.0 sigma (standard deviations)
6,210	defects for	4.0 sigma
233	defects for	5.0 sigma
3.4	defects for	6.0 sigma—no more than 3.4 defects per million opportunities (DPMO) or parts per million (PPM)

Rationale for Use

The establishment of six sigma quality would become a strong driving force to significantly increase customer satisfaction and would act as an enabler to reach world class status among competitors because:

- It promotes a common language and understanding of quality within the organization.
- It directly ties into a work ethic of TQM, IS0-9000, and integrated product development teams (IPDT).
- It assists in cost and cycle time reduction, waste elimination, and attacks variation at the supplier, process, product, and service level.
- It supports the Malcolm Baldrige National Quality Award criteria.

Procedures or Guidelines

The implementation of six sigma across the organization requires careful planning, effective training, and resource allocation for pilot studies, development of metrics, data collection/bases, and administrative procedures that include an organizational performance appraisal and reward system. The following reflect the basic steps:

- Communicate the six sigma quality strategy and roll-out plan. Start training core personnel.
- Define the organization's products and services.
- Identify suppliers and determine needs to be met.
- Determine desired customer characteristics and needs.
- Baseline processes for creating products and services. Establish metrics and procedures.
- Reduce variation, costs, cycle time, waste, and defects from the process.
- Measure results for continuous improvement.

Motorola's *Six Steps to Six Sigma Planning Guide* calls for:

1. Defining requirements
2. Identifying key traits
3. Analyzing variables that drive quality
4. Establishing target and tolerances
5. Measuring performance
6. Adjusting and controlling design and process

Related Metrics

Other statistical tools that can be directly linked to six sigma are:

- Process, results, and resource metrics
- Statistical process control (SPC) charts. These charts report on Cp, Cpk, FTY, DPU, DPMO, etc. *Example*: Stretch goal for 6σ (shifted), Cp = 2.00, Cpk = 1.50, DPMO = 3.4
- Inferential statistics: Null hypothesis (H_o) testing, probability testing, cost of quality, risk management
- Qualitative metrics for product value analysis and customer satisfaction
- Cycle time management (CTM), test and repair requirements analysis
- Parts standardization/management (PDM)

Application Examples

Regardless of organizational structure or function, six sigma quality can be considered for:

- New business development (proposals)
- Engineering (design changes/document errors)
- Manufacturing (rework/scrap costs)
- Finance (open accounts)
- Supply (inventory errors)
- Human resources (open requisitions)
- Customer service (complaint handling)
- Software programs/systems (lines of code)

Organizational Benefits

A key benefit from the establishment of—or from ongoing work to strive for six sigma quality—is the strategic alignment and much improved level of communications and teamwork among organizational units, and with the customer. Other more direct results are:

- Customer satisfaction and expanded market share
- Higher returns on resource expenditures
- Greatly enhanced engineering and manufacturing capability
- On-time delivery through cycle time reduction
- Cost reductions and improved financial results

Precautions and Considerations

Six sigma quality is not a short-term program but an ongoing and challenging process on the basis of a long-term performance plan. It must be interwoven with the organization's strategy and improvement goals at every level. It will require a significant amount of time and funding. A decision-making process must be in place to determine data collection and database administration costs, and also training needs from the "introduction" to the "product design" level. There must be criteria for key process selection because a small, incremental improvement in six sigma efforts may not justify the costs involved in bringing about process changes.

Use with Other TQM Tools

There are a number of tools that are presently in use and that complement six sigma:

- (DFMA) Design for Manufacturing and Assembly: Efficiency/lean manufacturing
- (DTC) Design to Costs: Cost reduction techniques
- (SPC) Statistical Process Control: Monitoring/tracking specification requirements
- (IPDT) Integrated Product Development Teams: Cross-functional product/service development
- (DOE) Design of Experiments: Robust design up front
- (CTM) Cycle Time Management: Cycle time reduction
- (QFD) Quality Function Deployment: The customer's voice in product design
- Basili Data Collection Model: Goal attainment and measurement
- (BM/T) Benchmarking/Trending: Best practices/processes
- (P-Y) Poke-Yoke: Mistake proofing the process
- (JIT) Just-in-time: Stockless, timely operations
- (MBP) Management by Policy: Hoshin planning process

Trends

The review of recent literature suggests an increasing trend by organizations to attain six sigma (6σ) quality (for example, Motorola, IBM, Texas Instruments, Hewlett Packard, Boeing).

This cross-reference alphabetically lists the 222 tools (as well as their aka's) as they appear in *Tool Navigator*™. Tool cross-references are in parentheses. Numerical designations, for example number **122**, indicate the tool number. Letter designations, for example (IG), indicate tool classification (Idea Generating). The tools in bold type include the tools in this book, as well as other problem-solving and creativity enhancing tools that may be typically used by cross-functional teams.

Tool Number in *40 Tools for Cross-Functional Teams*	Tool Number in *Tool Navigator*™		Tool Name
	1	**(IG)**	**5W2H method**
22	**2**	**(IG)**	**6-3-5 method**
			Abstraction process (*see* tool 102)
			Accountability grid (*see* tool 166)
			Action and consequences diagram (*see* tool 86)
	3	(AT)	Action and effect diagram (AED)
	4	(PP)	Action plan
	5	(AT)	Activity analysis
	6	(DC)	Activity cost matrix
	7	(PP)	Activity network diagram
			Affinity analysis (*see* tool 8)
15	**8**	**(IG)**	**Affinity diagram**
	9	**(IG)**	**Analogy and metaphor**
	10	(AT)	Analysis of variance
			ANOVA, F-test (*see* tool 10)
			Area graph (*see* tool 133)
			Arrow analysis (*see* tool 7)
			Assembly flow (*see* tool 221)
23	**11**	**(IG)**	**Attribute listing**
	12	(PP)	Audience analysis
	13	(DM)	Balance sheet
			Bar graph (*see* tool 14)
	14	(AT)	Bar chart
	15	(CI)	Barriers-and-aids analysis
	16	(PP)	Basili data collection method
	17	(DC)	Benchmarking
			Benefits and barriers exercise (*see* tool 15)
	18	(AT)	Block diagram
			Box and whisker plot (*see* tool 19)

Tool Number in *40 Tools for Cross-Functional Teams*	Tool Number in *Tool Navigator*™		Tool Name
	19	(AT)	Box plot
			Brain webs (*see* tool 110)
24	**20**	**(IG)**	**Brainstorming**
			Brainwriting (*see* tool 21)
	21	**(IG)**	**Brainwriting pool**
	22	(AT)	Breakdown tree
			Bulletin board fishbone (*see* tool 26)
16	**23**	**(TB)**	**Buzz group**
			Buzzing (*see* tool 23)
			Capability assessment chart (*see* tool 126)
			Capability indices (*see* tool 147)
			Case analysis method (*see* tool 24)
	24	(DC)	Case study
			Cause analysis (*see* tool 143)
	25	(AT)	Cause and effect diagram (CED)
	26	(AT)	Cause and effect diagram adding cards (CEDAC)
			Checkerboard diagram (*see* tool 27)
25	**27**	**(IG)**	**Checkerboard method**
	28	**(IG)**	**Checklist**
	29	(DC)	Checksheet
			Chi-square analysis (*see* tool 92)
			Circle chart (*see* tool 133)
26	**30**	**(IG)**	**Circle of opportunity**
	31	**(DC)**	**Circle response**
2	**32**	**(TB)**	**Circles of influence**
	33	**(DC)**	**Circles of knowledge**
27	**34**	**(IG)**	**Circumrelation**
	35	(ES)	Cluster analysis

Tool Number in *40 Tools for Cross-Functional Teams*	Tool Number in *Tool Navigator*™		Tool Name
			Clustering (*see* tool 35)
			Color code audit (*see* tool 103)
			Color dots rating (*see* tool 187)
			Comparative assessment matrix (*see* tool 36)
			Comparative benchmarking (*see* tool 17)
			Comparison grid (*see* tool 128)
	36	(ES)	Comparison matrix
	37	(AT)	Competency gap assessment
			Concentration diagram (*see* tool 60)
	38	(DC)	Conjoint analysis
17	**39**	**(DM)**	**Consensus decision making**
			Consensus generator (*see* tool 39)
	40	(AT)	Control Chart - c (attribute)
	41	(AT)	Control Chart - p (attribute)
	42	(AT)	Control Chart - $\bar{X}$-R (variable)
	43	(DM)	Correlation analysis
	44	(AT)	Cost of quality
			Cost of quality analysis (*see* tool 44)
	45	(ES)	Cost-benefit analysis
	46	(PP)	Countermeasures matrix
	47	**(IG)**	**Crawford slip method**
			Crawford slip writing (*see* tool 47)
			Creative evaluation (*see* tool 48)
38	**48**	**(ES)**	**Creativity assessment**
	49	(ES)	Criteria filtering
			Criteria ranking (*see* tool 159)
			Criteria rating (*see* tool 160)
			Criteria rating form (*see* tool 135)
18	**50**	**(IG)**	**Critical dialogue**
	51	(DC)	Critical incident
			Critical path method (CPM) (*see* tool 152)
			Cross-functional matrix (*see* tool 85)
			Cross-functional process map (*see* tool 150)
	52	(AT)	Customer acquisition-defection matrix
	53	(DC)	Customer needs table
	54	(AT)	Customer satisfaction analysis (CSA)
			Customer satisfier matrix (see tool 54)
			Customer window grid (*see* tool 178)
	55	(DC)	Customer-first-questions (CFQ)
	56	(AT)	Cycle time flowchart
			Daily operations log (*see* tool 71)
			Data collection plan (*see* tool 57)
	57	(DC)	Data collection strategy
			Data entry form (*see* tool 164)
			Data matrix (*see* tool 164)
			Decision flow analysis (*see* tool 59)
			Decision model (*see* tool 58)
	58	(DM)	Decision process flowchart
	59	(DM)	Decision tree diagram
			Defect location check-sheet (*see* tool 60)
	60	(DC)	Defect map
	61	**(ES)**	**Delphi method**
	62	(CI)	Deming PDSA cycle
			Deming wheel (*see* tool 62)
	63	**(AT)**	**Demographic analysis**
	64	(ES)	Dendrogram
	65	(PP)	Deployment chart (down-across)
	66	(PP)	Descriptive statistics
			Dialogue (*see* tool 50)
39	**67**	**(PP)**	**Different point of view**
			Dimension map (*see* tool 157)
	68	(PP)	Dimensions cube
			Direct association (*see* tool 81)
			Distribution ratio (*see* tool 133)

Tool Number in *40 Tools for Cross-Functional Teams*	Tool Number in *Tool Navigator*™		Tool Name
	69	(AT)	Dot diagram
			Dot plot (*see* tool 69)
28	**70**	**(IG)**	**Double reversal**
	71	(CI)	Events log
	72	(CI)	Facility layout diagram
	73	(ES)	Factor analysis
	74	(CI)	Failure mode effect analysis (FMEA)
	75	(AT)	Fault tree analysis (FTA)
			Fishbone diagram (*see* tool 25)
3	**76**	**(TB)**	**Fishbowls**
			Five w's and two h's (*see* tool 1)
	77	(AT)	Five whys
			Flow methods diagram (*see* tool 194)
	78	(DC)	Focus group
	79	(CI)	Fog index
	80	(CI)	Force field analysis (FFA)
29	**81**	**(IG)**	**Forced association**
	82	(DM)	Forced choice
			Forced comparison (*see* tool 82)
			Forced relationship method (*see* tool 34)
			Free association (*see* tool 30)
			Free-form brainstorming (*see* tool 20)
	83	(AT)	Frequency distribution (FD)
			Frequency table (*see* tool 83)
30	**84**	**(IG)**	**Fresh eye**
			Function block diagram (*see* tool 18)
	85	**(AT)**	**Functional map**
	86	(AT)	Futures wheel
			Futuring (*see* tool 86)
			Gallery method (*see* tool 21)
	87	(PP)	Gantt chart
			Gantt planning (*see* tool 87)
	88	(CI)	Gap analysis
			Gaussian curve (*see* tool 119)
			Goal planning (*see* tool 16)
	89	(PP)	Gozinto chart

Tool Number in *40 Tools for Cross-Functional Teams*	Tool Number in *Tool Navigator*™		Tool Name
			Gunning fog index (*see* tool 79)
	90	(AT)	Histogram
			Histogram analysis (*see* tool 90)
	91	(ES)	House of quality
			Hypothesis testing (ANOVA) (*see* tool 10)
	92	(DM)	Hypothesis testing (chi-square)
			Hypothesis testing (correlation) (*see* tool 43)
	93	**(ES)**	**Idea advocate**
31	**94**	**(IG)**	**Idea borrowing**
			Idea box (*see* tool 112)
	95	**(IG)**	**Idea grid**
			Imagery (*see* tool 108)
			Impact-effort analysis (*see* tool 49)
	96	**(DM)**	**Importance weighting**
			Incident analysis (*see* tool 51)
	97	(PP)	Influence diagram
	98	(DC)	Information needs analysis
			Input-output analysis (*see* tool 195)
			Instant priorities (*see* tool 120)
			Interaction diagram (*see* tool 182)
			Interaction-relations diagram (*see* tool 99)
	99	(AT)	Interrelationship digraph (I.D.)
	100	(DC)	Interview technique
			Interviewing (see tool 100)
			Ishikawa diagram (*see* tool 25)
			Job analysis (*see* tool 196)
			Jury of experts (*see* tool 61)
			K-J method (see tool 8)
			Line graph (*see* tool 101)
	101	(AT)	Line chart
			Link analysis (*see* tool 221)
	102	(ES)	Linking diagram
			List reduction (*see* tool 49)
			Logic diagram (*see* tool 58)
	103	(CI)	Major program status
	104	(AT)	Markov analysis

Tool Number in *40 Tools for Cross-Functional Teams*	Tool Number in *Tool Navigator*™		Tool Name
			Matrix chart (*see* tool 106)
	105	(ES)	Matrix data analysis
	106	(PP)	Matrix diagram
	107	(ES)	Measurement matrix
			Meeting process check (*see* tool 197)
32	108	(IG)	**Mental imaging**
			Metaphorical thinking (*see* tool 9)
	109	(PP)	Milestones chart
	110	(IG)	**Mind flow**
	111	(IG)	Monthly assessment schedule
33	112	(IG)	**Morphological analysis**
			Morphological forced connections (*see* tool 112)
			Multiple line graph (*see* tool 190)
	113	(DC)	Multiple rating matrix
			Multiple rating profile (*see* tool 113)
			Multi-var chart (*see* tool 114)
	114	(AT)	Multivariable chart
			Multi-vote technique (*see* tool 115)
	115	(DM)	**Multivoting**
	116	(AT)	Needs analysis
			Needs assessment (see tool 116)
			Network diagram (see tool 99)
			Node diagram (see tool 7)
			Nominal group process (*see* tool 117)
19	117	(IG)	**Nominal group technique (NGT)**
			Nominal grouping (*see* tool 117)
	118	(ES)	**Nominal prioritization**
	119	(AT)	Normal probability distribution
	120	(ES)	**Numerical prioritization**
	121	(CI)	Objectives matrix (OMAX)
	122	(DC)	Observation
	123	(ES)	**Opportunity analysis**
	124	(PP)	Organization chart
4	125	(TB)	**Organization mapping**
1	126	(CI)	**Organization readiness chart**

Tool Number in *40 Tools for Cross-Functional Teams*	Tool Number in *Tool Navigator*™		Tool Name
			Organizational mirror (*see* tool 198)
			Osborne brainstorming (*see* tool 20)
			Outsider's view (*see* tool 67)
20	127	(TB)	**Pair matching overlay**
	128	(ES)	**Paired comparison**
			Pairwise ranking (*see* tool 120)
	129	(AT)	Panel debate
			Pareto analysis (*see* tool 130)
	130	(AT)	Pareto chart
			Pareto principle (*see* tool 130)
			Partner link (*see* tool 127)
			Percent change bar graph (*see* tool 209)
			Performance gap analysis (*see* tool 37)
			Performance index (*see* tool 121)
			Perspective wheel (*see* tool 169)
21	131	(IG)	**Phillips 66**
			Phillips 66 buzz session (*see* tool 131)
			Pictogram (see tool 132)
	132	(PP)	Pictograph
	133	(AT)	Pie chart
	134	(IG)	**Pin cards technique**
			Plan-do-check-act strategy (*see* tool 180)
			Planning schedule (*see* tool 109)
21	135	(DM)	**Point-scoring evaluation**
	136	(AT)	Polygon
			Polygon analysis (*see* tool 136)
	137	(AT)	Polygon overlay
			Polygon trend comparison (*see* tool 137)
			Positive-negative chart (*see* tool 209)
	138	(CI)	Potential problem analysis (PPA)
40	139	(PP)	**Presentation**
			Presentation review (*see* tool 139)

Tool Number in *40 Tools for Cross-Functional Teams*	Tool Number in *Tool Navigator*™		Tool Name
	140	(ES)	Prioritization matrix—analytical
	141	(ES)	Prioritization matrix—combination
	142	(ES)	Prioritization matrix—consensus
	143	(AT)	Problem analysis
			Problem definition (*see* tool 145)
	144	(ES)	Problem selection matrix
			Problem solution planning (*see* tool 46)
12	**145**	**(PP)**	**Problem specification**
	146	(AT)	Process analysis
	147	(AT)	Process capability ratios
			Process cycle time analysis (*see* tool 56)
	148	(PP)	Process decision program chart (PDPC)
			Process flow analysis (*see* tool 149)
	149	(AT)	Process flowchart
13	**150**	**(CI)**	**Process mapping**
14	**151**	**(CI)**	**Process selection matrix**
	152	(PP)	Program evaluation and review technique (PERT)
	153	(PP)	Project planning log
	154	(ES)	Project prioritization matrix
			Pros and cons (*see* tool 13)
	155	(CI)	Quality chart
	156	(DC)	Questionnaires
	157	(AT)	Radar chart
	158	(DC)	Random numbers generator
			Random numbers table (*see* tool 158)
	159	(ES)	Ranking matrix
	160	(ES)	Rating matrix
			Recorded round robin technique (*see* tool 2)
5	**161**	**(TB)**	**Relationship map**
			Requirements matrix (*see* tool 163)
			Requirements QFD matrix (*see* tool 91)
	162	(PP)	Resource histogram
			Resource loading (*see* tool 162)
	163	**(PP)**	**Resource requirements matrix**

Tool Number in *40 Tools for Cross-Functional Teams*	Tool Number in *Tool Navigator*™		Tool Name
	164	(DC)	Response data encoding form
	165	(DC)	Response matrix analysis
10	**166**	**(CI)**	**Responsibility matrix**
			Results reporting (*see* tool 107)
	167	**(ES)**	**Reverse brainstorming**
			Reverse fishbone (*see* tool 3)
			Reversed thinking (*see* tool 70)
			Reviewed dendrogram (*see* tool 64)
			Risk management diagram (*see* tool 168)
	168	(AT)	Risk space analysis
			Root cause analysis (*see* tool 77)
			Rotating chairs (*see* tool 169)
11	**169**	**(CI)**	**Rotating roles**
	170	**(IG)**	**Round robin brainstorming**
	171	(AT)	Run chart
	172	**(AT)**	**Run-it-by**
			Sample analysis (*see* tool 22)
			Sampling (random/systematic/stratified/cluster) (*see* tool 173)
			Sampling chart (*see* tool 158)
	173	(DC)	Sampling methods
			Sarape chart (*see* tool 191)
34	**174**	**(AT)**	**SCAMPER**
			SCAMPER questions (*see* tool 174)
			Scatter analysis (*see* tool 175)
	175	(AT)	Scatter diagram
			Scatterplot (*see* tool 175)
			Scenario construction (*see* tool 176)
	176	(CI)	Scenario writing
			Second opinion (*see* tool 172)
			Selection grid (*see* tool 177)
	177	(ES)	Selection matrix
	178	(ES)	Selection window

Tool Number in *40 Tools for Cross-Functional Teams*	Tool Number in *Tool Navigator*™		Tool Name
35	179	(IG)	**Semantic intuition**
	180	(CI)	Shewhart PDCA cycle
			Situation analysis (*see* tool 193)
	181	(AT)	Snake chart
6	182	(TB)	**Sociogram**
			Sociometric diagram (*see* tool 182)
			Solution impact diagram (*see* tool 3)
	183	(ES)	Solution matrix
			Solutions selection matrix (*see* tool 183)
			Space plot (*see* tool 168)
			Spider chart (*see* tool 157)
	184	(AT)	Standard deviation
	185	(DC)	**Starbursting**
			Stem-and-leaf diagram (*see* tool 186)
	186	(AT)	Stem-and-leaf display
	187	(ES)	**Sticking dots**
36	188	(IG)	**Stimulus analysis**
			Storyboard (*see* tool 189)
	189	(PP)	Storyboarding
	190	(AT)	Stratification
	191	(AT)	Stratum chart
			Surface chart (*see* tool 191)
			Survey analysis (*see* tool 192)
			Survey profiling (*see* tool 165)
	192	(DC)	Surveying
	193	(PP)	SWOT analysis
	194	(AT)	Symbolic flowchart
			Systematic diagram (*see* tool 204)
	195	(AT)	Systems analysis diagram
			Tally sheet (*see* tool 29)
	196	(AT)	Task analysis
7	197	(TB)	**Team meeting evaluation**
8	198	(TB)	**Team mirror**
9	199	(TB)	**Team process assessment**
			Team rating (*see* tool 187)
			Teardown method (*see* tool 167)
	200	(AT)	Thematic content analysis
			Time plot (*see* tool 202)
			Time series analysis (*see* tool 205)

Tool Number in *40 Tools for Cross-Functional Teams*	Tool Number in *Tool Navigator*™		Tool Name
	201	(CI)	Time study sheet
	202	(AT)	Timeline chart
	203	(PP)	Top-down flowchart
			Traditional organization chart (*see* tool 124)
			Tree analysis (*see* tool 204)
	204	(PP)	Tree diagram
	205	(AT)	Trend analysis
	206	(ES)	**Triple ranking**
	207	(AT)	Truth table
			Two-dimensional scatter diagram (*see* tool 208)
	208	(DC)	Two-dimensional survey grid
	209	(AT)	Two-directional bar chart
	210	(AT)	Value analysis
	211	(AT)	Value/non-value-added cycle time chart
	212	(AT)	Variance analysis
			Variance matrix (*see* tool 212)
	213	(ES)	Venn diagram
			Visualization (*see* tool 108)
			Voice of the customer (*see* tool 53)
			Weighted averages matrix (*see* tool 96)
	214	(DM)	**Weighted voting**
	215	(AT)	**What-if analysis**
	216	(PP)	Why/how charting
37	217	(IG)	**Wildest idea technique**
			Wildest idea thinking (*see* tool 217)
	218	(AT)	Window analysis
	219	(AT)	**Wishful thinking**
			Work breakdown diagram (*see* tool 220)
	220	(PP)	Work breakdown structure (WBS)
	221	(CI)	Work flow analysis (WFA)
	222	(AT)	**Yield chart**

References

Albright, Mary, and Clay Carr. 1997. *101 Biggest Mistakes Managers Make*. Paramus, NJ: Prentice Hall.

Arieti, Silvano. 1976. *The Magic Synthesis*. New York, NY: Harper Collins Publishers.

Aubrey, Charles A. II, and Patricia K. Felkins. 1988. *Teamwork: Involving People in Quality and Productivity Improvement*. New York: Quality Resources.

Couger, J. Daniel. 1995. *Creative Problem Solving and Opportunity Finding*. New York: Boyd & Fraser Publishing Company.

Dessler, Gary. 1997. *Human Resource Management* (7th ed.). Upper Saddle River, NJ: Prentice-Hall, Inc.

Dyer, William G. 1987. *Team Building* (2nd ed.). Reading, MA: Addison-Wesley Publishing Company.

Evans, James R., and William M. Lindsay. 1996. *The Management and Control of Quality* (3rd ed.). St. Paul, MN: West Publishing Company.

Felkins, Patricia K., Kenneth N. Chakiris, and B.J. Chakiris. 1993. *Change Management*. White Plains, NY: Quality Resources.

Fisher, Kimball. 1993. *Leading Self-Directed Work Teams*. New York: McGraw-Hill, Inc.

Fogg, C. Davis. 1994. *Team-Based Strategic Planning*. New York, NY: AMACOM.

Francis, Dave, and Don Young. 1979. *Improving Work Groups*. San Diego, CA: University Associates, Inc.

Goodmeasure, Inc. (Staff). 1988. *Solving Quality and Productivity Problems*. Milwaukee, WI: ASQC Quality Press.

Harrington, James H. 1995. *Total Improvement Management*. New York: McGraw-Hill, Inc.

Harrington-Mackin, Deborah. 1994. *The Team Building Toolkit*. New York: AMACOM.

Harshman, Carl L., and Steven L. Phillips. 1994. *Teaming-Up*. San Diego, CA: Pfeiffer & Company.

Head, Christopher W. 1997. *Beyond Corporate Transformation*. Portland, OR: Productivity Press.

Hunt, V. Daniel. 1992. *Quality in America*. Burr Ridge, IL: Irwin Professional Publishing.

Kanter, Rosabeth Moss. 1989. "New Managerial Work." *Harvard Business Review* (November–December).

Katzenbach, Jon R., and Douglas K. Smith. 1993a. "The Discipline of Teams." *Harvard Business Review* (March–April).

Katzenbach, Jon R., and Douglas K. Smith. 1993b. *The Wisdom of Teams*. Boston, MA: Harvard Business School Press.

Kayser, Thomas A. 1994. *Building Team Power*. Burr Ridge, IL: Irwin Professional Publishing.

Kern, Annemarie. 1997. "No Team Is an Island." *ASQ Quality Progress* (May).

Kumar, Naga. 1998. Personal communication, May 2. Dr. Kumar is the president of Organizational Change Performance, Inc., 24016 Arminta Street, West Hills, CA 91304, telephone 818-888-2783, e-mail (Orgcp@aol.com).

McIntosh-Fletcher, Donna. 1996. *Teaming by Design*. Burr Ridge, IL: Irwin Professional Publishing.

Mankin, Don, Susan G. Cohen, and Tora K. Bikson. 1996. *Teams & Technology*. Boston, MA: Harvard Business School Press.

Michalski, Walter J. 1997. *Tool Navigator™—The Master Guide for Teams*. Portland, OR: Productivity Press, Inc.

Miller, William C. 1986. *The Creative Edge*. New York: Addison-Wesley Publishing Company, Inc.

Mundt, B.M. 1994. These team type designations were used by B. M. Mundt, KPHG Peat Marwick, at the IIE Conference, March 7.

Newman, Ruth G., and Bradford W. Ketchum, Jr. 1994. *Recruit, Motivate, & Lead Your Team: Managing People*. Boston, MA: Inc. Publishing.

Null, Steven R. 1998. Personal communication, April 29. Dr. Null is president of Pellennium, Inc., e-mail (Pellennium@aol.com).

Parker, Glenn M. 1994. *Cross-Functional Teams*. San Francisco, CA: Jossey-Bass, Inc.

Piczak, Mihael W., and Reuben Z. Hauser. 1996. "Self-Directed Work Teams: A Guide to Implementation." *ASQ Quality Progress* (May).

Rees, Fran. *How to Lead Work Teams*. 1991. San Fransisco, CA: Jossey-Bass/Pfeiffer.

Robbins, Harvey, and Michael Finley. 1995. *Why Teams Don't Work*. Princeton, NJ: Peterson's/Pacesetter Books.

Robie, Richard S. 1997. "Is Your Organization Spooked by Ghostly Team Performance?" *ASQ Quality Progress* (May).

Scholtes, Peter R. 1988. *The Team Handbook*. Madison, WI: Joiner Associates, Inc.

Senge, Peter M., Charlotte Roberts, Richard Ross, Bryan Smith, and Art Kleiner. 1994. *The Fifth Discipline Fieldbook*. New York: Currency Doubleday.

Sharpiro, Eileen. 1992. *How Corporate Truths Become Competitive Traps*. Carlsbad, CA: CRM Films.

Sherriton, Jacalyn, and James L. Stern. 1997. *Corporate Culture—Team Culture*. New York: AMACOM.

Shonk, James H. 1992. *Team-Based Organizations*. Homewood, IL: Business One Irwin.

Stewart, John Parker. 1994. *Corporate Performance & Employee Commitment—Inverting the Pyramid*. Des Moines, IA: Excellence in Training Corp.

Tuckman, B.W., and M.A.C. Jenson. 1992. *Group and Organization Studies*. American Society for Training and Development.

Tucker, Jerold V. 1998. Personal communication, April 20. Mr. Tucker is assistant vice president of *Learning Solutions, GTE*.

Wellins, Richard S., William C. Byham, and Jeanne M. Wilson. 1991. *Empowered Teams*. San Francisco, CA: Jossey-Bass Publishers.

Willcocks, Graham, and Steve Morris. 1997. *Successful Team Building*. Hauppage, NY: Barron's Educational Series, Inc.

Willingham, Ron. 1997. *The People Principle*. New York: St. Martin's Press.

Zenger, John H., Ed Musselwhite, Kathleen Hurson, and Craig Perrin. 1994. *Leading Teams*. Burr Ridge, IL: Irwin Professional Publishing.

Abbreviated Bibliography

Bechtell, Michele L. *Untangling Organizational Gridlock*. Milwaukee, WI: ASQC Quality Press, 1993.

Beck, John D. W., and Neil M. Yeager. "Team Work: How to Prevent Teams from Failing." *ASQ Quality Progress* (March 1996).

Bolton, Robert. *People Skills*. New York: Simon & Schuster, Inc., 1979.

Boshear, Walton C., and Karl G. Albrecht. *Understanding People: Models and Concepts*. San Diego, CA: University Associates Inc., 1977.

Butler, Ava S. *Team Think*. New York, NY: McGraw-Hill Inc., 1996.

Davenport, Thomas H. *Process Innovation*. Boston, MA: Harvard Business School Press, 1993.

Davis, Duane, and Robert M. Cosenza. *Business Research for Decision Making* (3rd ed.). Belmont, CA: Wadsworth Publishing Company, 1993.

De Bono, Edward. *Chancen: Das Trainingsmodell fuer erfolgreiche Ideensuche*. Duesseldorf, Germany: ECON Taschenbuch Verlag GmbH, 1991.

De Bono, Edward. *Laterales Denken*. Duesseldorf, Germany: ECON Verlag, 1989.

Deeprose, Donna. *The Team Coach*. New York: AMACOM, 1995.

Delbecq, A. L., A. H. Van de Ven, and D. H. Gustafson. *Group Techniques for Program Planning*. Glenview, IL: Scott, Foresman, 1975

Donovan, J. Michael. *Self Directed Work Teams*. Spartanburg, SC: AQP Association for Quality and Participation (Video-2000, Inc.), 1990.

Edwards, Paul, Sarah Edwards, and Rick Benzel. *Teaming Up*. New York, NY: Putnam Publishing Group, 1997.

Foy, Nancy. *Empowering People at Work*. Brockfield, VT: Gower, 1994.

Geschka, H. "*Methods and Organization or Idea Generation*." Paper presented at Creativity Week II, Center for Creative Leadership, Greensboro, NC, Sept. 1979.

Gross, Steven E. (Hay Group). *Compensation for Teams*. New York, NY: AMACOM, 1995.

Hackman, Richard J. "The Design of Work Teams," in J.W. Lorsch (ed.), *Handbook of Organizational Behavior*. Englewood Cliffs, NJ: Prentice-Hall, 1987.

Harrington, James H. *The Improvement Process*. Milwaukee, WI: Quality Press, 1987.

Harry, Mikel J. *The Nature of Six Sigma Quality*. Government Electronics Group, Motorola, Inc., 1987.

Heerman, Barry. *Building Team Spirit*. New York, NY: McGraw-Hill, Inc., 1997.

Henry, Jane E. "Lessons from Team Leaders." *ASQ Quality Progress* (March 1998).

Henry, Jane E., and Meg Hartzler. *Tools for Virtual Teams*. Milwaukee, WI: ASQ Quality Press, 1998.

Hughes Aircraft Company. *Guide for Integrated Product Development*. Los Angeles, CA: Hughes A&D Sector, 1993.

Jones, Morgan D. *The Thinker's Toolkit*. New York: Random House, Inc., 1995.

Kirby, Gary, and Jeffery R. Goodpaster. *Thinking*. Englewood Cliffs, NJ: Prentice-Hall, Inc., 1995.

Masaaki, Imai. *Kaizen*. New York: The Kaizen Institute, 1986.

Meyer, Christopher. "How the Right Measures Help Teams Excel." *Harvard Business Review* (May–June 1994).

Michalko, Michael. *Thinkertoys*. Berkeley, CA: Ten Speed Press, 1991.

Michalski, Walter J. *Tools and Notes*. Unpublished collection of approximately 500 tools and techniques for quality and process improvement, collection period 1965–1997.

Michalski, Walter J. *Tools for Teams: Hands-On Problem Solving and Process Improvement Manual*. Huntington Beach, CA: Alpha Research Group, 1994.

Nadler, Gerald, and Shozo Hibino. *Breakthrough Thinking*. Rocklin, CA: Prima Publishing, 1990.

Newstrom, John W. *Still More Games Trainers Play*. New York: McGraw-Hill, Inc., 1991.

Osborn, Jack D., et al. *Self-Directed Work Teams: The New American Challenge.* Homewood, IL: Business One Irwin, 1990.

Parker, Glenn M. *Team Players and Teamwork.* San Francisco, CA: Jossey-Bass Publishers, 1990.

Pfeiffer, J. William, and John E. Jones (eds.). *Handbook of Structured Experiences for Human Relations Training* (Vol. 1–10). San Diego, CA: University Associates, 1974–1990.

Pfeiffer, J. William (ed.). The *1972–1995 Annual Handbooks for Group Facilitators/Developing Human Resources.* San Diego, CA: University Associates, 1972–1991, Pfeiffer & Company, 1992–1995.

Prince, George M. *The Practice of Creativity.* New York: Macmillan Publishing Company, Inc., 1970.

Romig, Dennis A. *Breakthrough Teamwork.* Burr Ridge, IL: Irwin Professional Publishing, 1996.

Rubinstein, Moshe F. *Tools for Thinking and Problem Solving.* Englewood Cliffs, NJ: Prentice-Hall, Inc., 1986.

Rummler-Brache Group. *Introduction to Process Improvement and Management.* Warren, NJ: The Rummler-Brache Group, 1994.

Saaty, Thomas L. *Decision Making for Leaders.* University of Pittsburgh, 1988.

Swanson, Roger C. *The Quality Improvement Handbook.* Delray Beach, FL: St. Lucie Press, 1995.

Tague, Nancy R. *The Quality Toolbox.* Milwaukee, WI: ASQC Quality Press, 1995.

Utterback, James M. *Mastering the Dynamics of Innovation.* Boston, MA: Harvard Business School Press, 1994.

Van Gundy, Arthur B. *Techniques of Structured Problem-Solving.* New York: Van Nostrand Reinhold Company, 1981.

Vogt, Judith F., and Kenneth L. Murrell. *Empowerment in Organizations.* San Diego, CA: University Associates, Inc., 1990.

Wellins, Richard S., William C. Byham, and George R. Dixon. *Inside Teams.* Bridgeville, PA: Development Dimensions International, 1996.

Wetlaufer, Suzy. "The Team That Wasn't." *Harvard Business Review* (Nov-Dec 1994).

About the Author

Dr. Walter J. Michalski is president of Alpha Research Group, Huntington Beach, California, a TQM consulting firm that assists organizations in their quality and change initiatives. His work experience reflects 30 years in quality assurance, test/process engineering, and process improvement training. He has designed many problem-solving workshops and facilitated teams on quality issues, process reengineering, continuous improvement, measurement, organizational change, and critical-thinking techniques. Presently he facilitates customized Tool Navigator workshops designed for team facilitators/trainers to effectively and appropriately select and use any of the 222 tools listed in the *Tool Navigator*™—*A Master Guide for Teams*, also published by Productivity Press, Inc.

Dr. Michalski holds an Ed.D. in Institutional Management from Pepperdine University, GSEP, Los Angeles, California. His doctoral dissertation examined the effectiveness of nontraditional college degree programs. As an adjunct professor, he continues to teach at graduate and undergraduate levels in subjects such as research methods, statistics, TQM/TQS, management, and organizational behavior. He also serves as project advisor for students' research projects, practicums, and theses. He can be reached at Alpha Research Group, 8481 Ivy Circle, Huntington Beach, CA 92646. Tel/Fax: 714-968-0452, e-mail: WMichalski@earthlink.net.

Books from Productivity Press

Productivity Press publishes books that empower individuals and companies to achieve excellence in quality, productivity, and the creative involvement of all employees. Through steadfast efforts to support the vision and strategy of continuous improvement, Productivity Press delivers today's leading-edge tools and techniques gathered directly from industry leaders around the world. Call toll-free (800) 394-6868 for our free catalog.

20 Keys to Workplace Improvement (Revised Edition)
Iwao Kobayashi

The 20 Keys system does more than just bring together twenty of the world's top manufacturing improvement approaches—it integrates these individual methods into a closely interrelated system for revolutionizing every aspect of your manufacturing organization. This revised edition of Kobayashi's bestseller amplifies the synergistic power of raising the levels of all these critical areas simultaneously. The new edition presents upgraded criteria for the five-level scoring system in most of the 20 Keys, supporting your progress toward becoming not only best in your industry but best in the world.
ISBN 1-56327-109-5 / 302 pages / $50.00 / Order 20KREV-B8007

40 Top Tools for Manufacturers
A Guide for Implementing Powerful Improvement Activities
Walter Michalski

We know how important it is for you to have the right tool when you need it. And if you're a team leader or facilitator in a manufacturing environment, you've probably been searching a long time for a collection of implementation tools tailored specifically to your needs. Well, look no further. Based on the same principles and user-friendly design of the Tool Navigator's *The Master Guide for Teams*, here is a group of 40 dynamic tools to help you and your teams implement powerful manufacturing process improvement. Use this essential resource to select, sequence, and apply major TQM tools, methods, and processes.
ISBN 1-56327-197-4 / 160 pages / $25.00 / Order NAV2-B8007

The Benchmarking Management Guide
American Productivity & Quality Center

If you're planning, organizing, or actually undertaking a benchmarking program, you need the most authoritative source of information to help you get started and to manage the process all the way through. Written expressly for managers of benchmarking projects by the APQC's renowned International Benchmarking Clearinghouse, this guide provides exclusive information from members who have already paved the way. It includes information on training courses and ways to apply Baldrige, Deming, and ISO 9000 criteria for internal assessment, and has a complete bibliography of benchmarking literature.
ISBN 1-56327-045-5 / 260 pages / $40.00 / Order BMG-B8007

Beyond Corporate Transformation
A Whole Systems Approach to Creating and Sustaining High Performance
Christopher W. Head

When do your employees resist change? They resist change when they don't understand the changes that are taking place, they see little or no perceived benefit of doing things differently, or they do not feel involved. Which is why employees who will be affected by a transformation must effect the changes. Realizing that anything short of total employee involvement in the change process jeopardizes success, this book emphasizes that it is the responsibility of every employee to act as a change agent. Learn how to go beyond piece meal incremental changes, beyond reengineering, beyond the limited idea of change to encompass a whole systems approach to creating and sustaining a competitive advantage. Through a revolutionary, integrated, employee-oriented leadership philosophy, this book illustrates how to transform an organization by tapping into the full potential of every employee.

ISBN 1-56327-176-1 / 240 pages / $35.00 / Order BEYOND-B8007

Building Organizational Fitness
Management Methodology for Transformation and Strategic Advantage
Ryuji Fukuda

The most urgent task for companies today is to take a hard look at the future. To remain competitive, management must nurture a strong capability for self-development and a strong corporate culture, both of which form part of the foundation for improvement. But simply understanding management techniques doesn't mean you know how to use them. You need the tools and technologies for implementation. In *Building Organizational Fitness*, Fukuda extends the power of his managerial engineering methodology into the context of the top management strategic planning role.

ISBN 1-56327-144-3 / 250 pages / $65.00 / Order BFIT-B8007

Caught in the Middle
A Leadership Guide for Partnership in the Workplace
Rick Maurer

Managers today are caught between old skills and new expectations. You're expected not only to improve quality and services, but also to get staff more involved. This stimulating book provides the inspiration and know-how to achieve these goals as it brings to light the rewards of establishing a real partnership with your staff. Includes self-assessment questionnaires.

ISBN 1-56327-158-3 / 258 pages / $30.00 / Order CAUGHT-B8007

CEDAC
A Tool for Continuous Systematic Improvement
Ryuji Fukuda

CEDAC, encompasses three tools for continuous systematic improvement: window analysis (for identifying problems), the CEDAC diagram (a modification of the classic "fishbone diagram," for analyzing problems and developing standards), and window development (for ensuring adherence to standards). This manual provides directions for setting up and using CEDAC. Sample forms included.

ISBN 1-56327-140-0 / 144 pages / $30.00 / Order CEDAC-B8007

Feedback Toolkit
16 Tools for Better Communication in the Workplace
Rick Maurer

In companies striving to reduce hierarchy and foster trust and responsible participation, good person-to-person feedback can be as important as sophisticated computer technology in enabling effective teamwork. Feedback is an important map of your situation, a way to tell

whether you are "on or off track." Used well, feedback can motivate people to their highest level of performance. Despite its significance, this level of information sharing makes most managers uncomfortable. *Feedback Toolkit* addresses this natural hesitation with an easy-to-grasp 6-step framework and 16 practical and creative approaches for giving and receiving feedback with individuals and groups.
ISBN 1-56327-056-0 / 109 pages / $12.00 / Order FEED-B8007

Go-Go Tools
Five Essential Activities for Leading Small Groups
Shigehiro Nakamura and Hideyuki Takahashi

Small-group activities are an extremely important element of individual and organizational development, both stretching an employee's abilities and boosting your company's achievements. This exciting new book gives you a concise and creative set of tools to clearly establish management objectives and then helps you connect these objectives with your employees through self-directed work teams. Use this energizing guide to breathe new life into your small group activities and increase the effectiveness of your teams, meetings, and improvement processes.
ISBN 1-56327-200-8 / 110 pages / $25.00 / Order GOGO-B8007

Handbook for Personal Productivity
Henry E. Liebling

A little book with a lot of power that will help you become more successful and satisfied at work, as well as in your personal life. This pocket-sized handbook offers sections on personal productivity improvement, team achievement, quality customer service, improving your health, and how to get the most out of workshops and seminars. Special bulk discounts are available (call for more information).
ISBN 1-56327-131-1 / 128 pages / $5.00 paper / Order PERS-B8007

Handbook for Productivity Measurement and Improvement
William F. Christopher and Carl G. Thor, eds.

An unparalleled resource! In over 100 chapters, nearly 80 front-runners in the quality movement reveal the evolving theory and specific practices of world class organizations. Spanning a wide variety of industries and business sectors, they discuss quality and productivity in manufacturing, service industries, profit centers, administration, nonprofit and government institutions, health care and education. Contributors include Robert C. Camp, Peter F. Drucker, Jay W. Forrester, Joseph M. Juran, Robert S. Kaplan, John W. Kendrick, Yasuhiro Monden, and Lester C. Thurow. Comprehensive in scope and organized for easy reference, this compendium belongs in every company and academic institution concerned with business and industrial viability.
ISBN 1-56327-007-2 / 1344 pages / $90.00 / Order HPM-B8007

The Hunters and the Hunted
A Non-Linear Solution for Reengineering the Workplace
James B. Swartz

Our competitive environment changes rapidly. If you want to survive, you have to stay on top of those changes. Otherwise, you become prey to your competitors. Hunters continuously change and learn; anyone who doesn't becomes the hunted and sooner or later will be devoured. This unusual non-fiction novel provides a veritable crash course in continuous transformation. It offers lessons from real-life companies and introduces many industrial gurus as characters. The

Hunters and the Hunted doesn't simply tell you how to change; it puts you inside the change process itself.
ISBN 1-56327-043-9 / 564 pages / $45.00 / Order HUNT-Bxxx
ISBN 1-56327-043-9 / $19.95 / Order HUNTP-B8007

The Improvement Engine
Creativity and Innovation Through Employee Involvement—The Kaizen Teian System
JHRA (ed.)

The Improvement Engine offers the most all inclusive information available today on this proven method for increasing employee involvement. Kaizen Teian is a technique developed in Japan for encouraging employees to constantly look for and make improvement suggestions. This book explores the subtleties between designing a moderately successful program and a highly successful one and includes a host of tools, techniques, and case studies.
ISBN 1-56327-010-2 / 195 pages / $40.00 / Order IMPENG-B8007

Kaizen Teian 1
Developing Systems for Continuous Improvement Through Employee Suggestions
Japan Human Relations Association (ed.)

Especially relevant for middle and upper managers, this book focuses on the role of managers as catalysts in spurring employee ideas and facilitating their implementation. It explains how to run a proposal program on a day-to-day basis and outlines the policies that support a "bottom-up" system of innovation and defines the three main objectives of kaizen teian: to build participation, develop individual skills, and achieve higher profits.
ISBN 1-56327-186-9/ 217 pages / $30.00 / Order KT1P-B8007

Kaizen Teian 2
Guiding Continuous Improvement Through Employee Suggestions
Japan Human Relations Association (ed.)

Building on the concepts covered in *Kaizen Teian* I, this second volume examines in depth how to implement kaizen teian—a continuous improvement suggestions system. Managers will learn techniques for getting employees to think creatively about workplace improvements and how to run a successful proposal program.
ISBN 0-915299-53-4 / 221 pages / $30.00 / Order KT2P-B8007

Modeling for Learning Organizations
John Morecroft and John Sterman, eds.

An outstanding compilation of articles by top system dynamics thinkers worldwide, offering a "user-friendly" introduction to leading edge methods of organization modeling and answers to many of the questions raised by Peter Senge's best-selling book *The Fifth Discipline*. Part 1 discusses generally how modeling can support management decision making. Parts 2 and 3 offer case studies. Part 4 evaluates the latest software technology for computer simulation modeling.
ISBN 1-56327-060-9 / 426 pages / price $45.00 / Order XMLO-B8007

A New American TQM
Four Practical Revolutions in Management
Shoji Shiba, Alan Graham, and David Walden

For TQM to succeed in America, you need to create an American-style "learning organization" with the full commitment and understanding of senior managers and executives. Written expressly for this audience, *A New American TQM* offers a comprehensive and detailed explanation of TQM and how to implement it, based on courses taught at MIT's Sloan School of Management and the Center for Quality Management, a consortium of American companies. Full of case studies and amply illustrated, the book examines major quality tools and how they are being used by the most progressive American companies today.
ISBN 1-56327-032-3 / 598 pages / $50.00 / Order NATQM-B8007

Secrets of a Successful Employee Recognition System
Daniel C. Boyle

As the human resource manager of a failing manufacturing plant, Dan Boyle was desperate to find a way to motivate employees and break down the barrier between management and the union. He came up with a simple idea to say thank you to your employees for doing their job. In *Secrets to a Successful Employee Recognition System*, Boyle outlines how to begin and run a 100 Club program. Filled with case studies and detailed guidelines, this book underscores the power behind thanking your employees for a job well done.
ISBN 1-56327-083-8 / 250 pages / $25.00 / Order SECRET-B8007

Thoughtware
Change the Thinking and the Organization Will Change Itself
J. Philip Kirby & D.H. Hughes

In order to facilitate true change in an organization, its thinking patterns need to be the first thing to change. Your employees need more than empowerment. They need to move from doing their jobs to doing whatever is needed for the good of the entire organization. Thoughtware is the underlying platform on which every organization operates, the set of assumptions upon which the organization is structured. When you understand and change thoughtware, the tools and techniques of continuous improvement become incredibly powerful.
ISBN 1-56327-106-0 / 200 pages / $35.00 / Order THOUG-B8007

Tool Navigator
The Master Guide for Teams
Walter J. Michalski

Are you constantly searching for just the right tool to help your team efforts? Do you find yourself not sure which to use next? Here's the largest tool compendium of facilitation and problem solving tools you'll find. Each tool is presented in a two to three page spread which describes the tool, its use, how to implement it, and an example. Charts provide a matrix to help you choose the right tool for your needs. Plus, you can combine tools to help your team navigate through any problem solving or improvement process. Use these tools for all seasons: team building, idea generating, data collecting, analyzing/trending, evaluating/selecting, decision making, planning/presenting, and more!
ISBN 1-56327-178-8 / 550 pages / $150.00 / Order NAV1-B8007

The Unshackled Organization
Facing the Challenge of Unpredictability Through Spontaneous Reorganization
Jeffrey Goldstein
Managers should not necessarily try to solve all the internal problems within their organizations; intervention may help in the short term, but in the long run may inhibit true problem-solving change from taking place. And change is the real goal. Through change comes real hope for improvement. Using leading-edge scientific and social theories about change, Goldstein explores how change happens within an organization and reveals that only through "self-organization" can natural, lasting change occur. This book is a pragmatic guide for managers, executives, consultants, and other change agents.
ISBN 1-56327-048-X / 202 pages / $25.00 / Order UO-B8007

TO ORDER: Write, phone, or fax Productivity Press, Dept. BK, P.O. Box 13390, Portland, OR 97213-0390, phone 1-800-394-6868, fax 1-800-394-6286.

Outside the U.S. phone (503) 235-0600; fax (503) 235-0909

Send check or charge to your credit card (American Express, Visa, MasterCard accepted).

U.S. ORDERS: Add $5 shipping for first book, $2 each additional for UPS surface delivery. Add $5 for each AV program containing 1 or 2 tapes; add $12 for each AV program containing 3 or more tapes. We offer attractive quantity discounts for bulk purchases of individual titles; call for more information.

ORDER BY E-MAIL: Order 24 hours a day from anywhere in the world. Use either address:
To order: **service@ppress.com**
To view the online catalog and/or order: **http://www.ppress.com/**

QUANTITY DISCOUNTS: For information on quantity discounts, please contact our sales department.

INTERNATIONAL ORDERS: Write, phone, or fax for quote and indicate shipping method desired. For international callers, telephone number is 503-235-0600 and fax number is 503-235-0909. Prepayment in U.S. dollars must accompany your order (checks must be drawn on U.S. banks). When quote is returned with payment, your order will be shipped promptly by the method requested.

NOTE: Prices are in U.S. dollars and are subject to change without notice.

About the Shopfloor Series

Put powerful and proven improvement tools in the hands of your entire workforce!

Progressive shopfloor improvement techniques are imperative for manufacturers who want to stay competitive and to achieve world class excellence. And it's the comprehensive education of all shopfloor workers that ensures full participation and success when implementing new programs. The Shopfloor Series books make practical information accessible to everyone by presenting major concepts and tools in simple, clear language and at a reading level that has been adjusted for operators by skilled instructional designers. One main idea is presented every two to four pages so that the book can be picked up and put down easily. Each chapter begins with an overview and ends with a summary section. Helpful illustrations are used throughout.

Books currently in the Shopfloor Series include:

5S for Operators
5 Pillars of the Visual Workplace
The Productivity Press Development Team
ISBN 1-56327-123-0 /
incl. applic. questions / 133 pages
Order 5SOP-B8007 / $25.00

Quick Changeover for Operators
The SMED System
The Productivity Press Development Team
ISBN 1-56327-125-7 /
incl. applic. questions / 93 pages
Order QCOOP-B8007 / $25.00

Mistake-Proofing for Operators
The Productivity Press Development Team
ISBN 1-56327-127-3 / 93 pages
Order ZQCOP-B8007 / $25.00

TPM for Supervisors
The Productivity Press Development Team
ISBN 1-56327-161-3 / 96 pages
Order TPMSUP-B8007 / $25.00

TPM Team Guide
Kunio Shirose
ISBN 1-56327-079-X / 175 pages
Order TGUIDE-B8007 / $25.00

TPM for Every Operator
Japan Institute of Plant Maintenance
ISBN 1-56327-080-3 / 136 pages
Order TPMEO-B8007 / $25.00

Autonomous Maintenance
Japan Institute of Plant Maintenance
ISBN 1-56327-082-X / 138 pages
Order AUTMOP-B8007 / $25.00

Focused Equipment Improvement
Japan Institute of Plant Maintenance
ISBN 1-56327-081-1 / 138 pages
Order FEIOP-B8007 / $25.00

Just-in-Time for Operators
The Productivity Press Development Team
ISBN 1-56327-133-8 / 84 pages
Order JITOP-B8007 / $25.00

Continue Your Learning with In-House Training and Consulting from the Productivity Consulting Group

The Productivity Consulting Group (PCG) offers a diverse menu of consulting services and training products based on the exciting ideas contained in the books of Productivity Press. Whether you need assistance with long term planning or focused, results-driven training, PCG's experienced professional staff can enhance your pursuit of competitive advantage.

PCG integrates a cutting edge management system with today's leading process improvement tools for rapid, measurable, lasting results. In concert with your management team, PCG will focus on implementing the principles of Value Adding Management, Total Quality Management, Just-In-Time, and Total Productive Maintenance. Each approach is supported by Productivity's wide array of team-based tools: Standardization, One-Piece Flow, Hoshin Planning, Quick Changeover, Mistake-Proofing, Kanban, Problem Solving with CEDAC, Visual Workplace, Visual Office, Autonomous Maintenance, Equipment Effectiveness, Design of Experiments, Quality Function Deployment, Ergonomics, and more. And, based on the continuing research of Productivity Press, PCG expands its offering every year.

Productivity is known for significant improvement on the shopfloor and the bottom line. Through years of repeat business, an expanding and loyal client base continues to recommend Productivity to their colleagues. Contact PCG to learn how we can tailor our services to fit your needs.

Telephone: 1-800-966-5423 (U.S. only) or 1-203-846-3777
Fax: 1-203-846-6883